HERE FOR THE PRESENT

A *Grammar of Happiness in the Present Imperfect, Live, from the Poet's Perch*

Pacific Grove Poet-in-Residence
Barbara Mossberg
Sophia Mossberg, Illustrations

PACIFIC GROVE BOOKS
Pacific Grove, California

Here for the Present, A Grammar of Happiness in the Present Imperfect,
Live, from the Poet's Perch
Barbara Mossberg
Illustrations by Sophia Mossberg
Cover design by Janet Marcroft
Text design by Patricia Hamilton

© 2021 Text, Barbara Mossberg—© 2021 Images, © Sophia Mossberg
FIRST EDITION July 2021
PRINT - ISBN 978-1-953120-14-4
E-book - ISBN 978-1-053120-44-1

PACIFIC GROVE BOOKS
An imprint of
Park Place Publications
Pacific Grove, CA
pacificgrovebooks.com

A donation is made to the Friends of the
Pacific Grove Library for every book sold.

To Nicolino

here when this book began, an infinite presence, present

And To
You—Here—in the now, for now—A Gift

With immense gratitude, to Pacific Grove,
founded and carrying on in the spirit of poetry,
a shining fractal of the world community
in which poetry is a civic treasure
– Barbara Mossberg

"We can only be said to be alive in those moments when our hearts
are conscious of our treasures."
– Thornton Wilder

"events must be sung and sing themselves"
– Emerson

"and today is a gift, that is why it is called the present"
– Eleanor Roosevelt

When consciousness is sung
Events become eventful
A moment becomes momentous
Wonder makes a wonderland
A world that is wonderful
We see and do not take for granted—
You who are here
Making presence a present, a gift, a treasure

CONTENTS
HERE FOR THE PRESENT

Part One
MOMENTS

The Sun Rose—and other everyday curious happenings

In which you're an amateur at residence, aflutter as the Monarchs—warming up sketches trying to figure out sky and mirror messaging, and where hunger takes you

Part Two
FIELD WORK

In which I aspire to walk like a Camel, or however morning is supposed to come, walking a mile in Thoreau's shoes

Part Three
THE PLEIN AIR MIND

In which we consider simplicity as ecstasy in washing dishes, naked forest running and jumping into lakes, and other lessons of light from *The Physics of Purple* and Other Memories in the Present Perfect

Part Four
PRESENCE OF MIND

In which we learn how to *establish the pond*

Part Five

THE PERFECT IMPERFECT
OF QUANTUM HAPPINESS

In which we unwrap the time-space conundrum when your mother is in hospice, your father is eyeing angels—oh, only as an artist, your husband has cancer, your children text you at 2 am, neighbors kill your tree, a bear is loose and you are worried, your students worry, you want to cook for everyone, and life on land and sea goes on, with wings

Part Six
PRESENTS OF MIND
In which the present imperfect presents itself

A WORD AT THE END
How a city made poetry its business and a house a poet's perch, and a poet said in council chambers, "Pinch me!"

present imperfect — *Wiktionary*

Past continuous
The imperfect is a verb form which combines past tense and imperfective aspect. It can have meanings similar to the English "was walking" or "used to walk." It contrasts with preterite forms, which refer to a single completed event in the past.

The **present imperfect** tense is used for actions that are performed regularly or often, or for statements about an existing condition. It is also sometimes called the **present** habitual tense. Examples: I go to school. They eat vegetables.

EnglishEdit. NounEdit · **present imperfect** (uncountable). A grammatical tense which presents the action in the present as continuous, not yet over.

Prologue

Poetry is not a city's business. You might say that as a reasonable person, unless you knew about Pacific Grove. The City of Pacific Grove, more undersea than land, a spit, an outcropping, a knuckly thrust along the Pacific Coast splashed by seas where whales and otters and seals find home, where monarch butterflies imitate leaves, and wheelbarrows and ladders for sale are propped on the sidewalk across from City Hall, is less city than intentional village. It began as an encampment, founded out of a belief that sitting under trees and sky engenders spiritual and intellectual thinking that challenge a community to be civically vibrant. The actual fabric tents for the resident Chautauqua programs became Victorian "tents" – houses built on the original tent foundations, and out of such tents, poetry and art and literature sprang up.

A few blocks from where John Steinbeck lived, a poet named Whitney Latham Lechich was so grateful for this artsy ethos that she put her money where her mouth was: she left her house on 18th Street, right up from Lovers Point, to the City, as a place to promote poetry. It was called "The Poet's Perch." In 2010 I answered a call, notified of the possibility by Glinda Anderson, a massage therapist on Lighthouse, a gift to me from my director in Lettice and Lovage, the renowned Rosemary Luke, to be the City's Poet in Residence. I had to audition for representatives of the City: The City Cultural Commission, newspaper publisher of the Cedar Street Times, Mayor's office, city schools, and business and civic leaders. Pacific Grove was on a scale that could realistically make possible my aspiration: "no place safe from poetry." It was walkable in an hour if you took your time. I charged into the room quoting the Librarian of Congress, U.S. Laureate Mark Strand,

> Ink runs from the corners of my mouth.
> There is no happiness like mine.
> I have been eating poetry. ("Eating Poetry")

How can you go wrong invoking lines like that?

I moved into the Poet's Perch, as wide as a hug. I lived there for five years and continue to write from there in my mind. The opportunity to serve Pacific Grove as its Poet in Residence was a vibrational experience. The Mayor's office, Carnegie public library, Jewell Park's Little House and pagoda, schools, retirement homes, bookstores, art galleries, and businesses, were enablers of shenanigans, hosting me and playing a role in programs enacting the idea that poetry is necessary in our lives. The community rallied around writing and reading poetry. There were Flash Mobs on Cannery Row with Pacific Grove High School students chanting Emily Dickinson's "I'm Nobody!" Passersby murmured, "me, too!" Sixth graders on the threshold of the teenage journey spent two full school- days devoted to sonnet writing as problem solving. Art gallery openings were "Occupied" by citizens quoting Pablo Neruda. The library hosted writing workshops, Emily Dickinson's birthday readings, Persian New Year, art installations commissioning art around the world inspired by Emily Dickinson's poetry, California Laureate programs joining artists and poets; there were lectures at Chautauqua Hall, and around town, programs for Arbor Day, Earth Day, John Muir's birthday, Peace Lantern Ceremonies, Return of the Monarchs. Poetry was read at City Hall meetings. People gathered in the Jewell Park Gazebo for Poetry and Music and Poetry and Clowns. The Little House in Jewell Park hosted monthly poetry gatherings of Poetry in the

Grove Grove on figures ranging from Rumi to Gary Snyder.
Poetry was a daily disruption, intervention, disturbance, and poke in city life.

Pacific Grove was always known as a hotbed for creativity in line with the spheres, and when the new U.S. Poet Laureate was inaugurated at the Library of Congress, W.S. Merwin, I went to represent us and America's cities in general and present a plaque from the City for the occasion. I was "here to present!" Recently when I was serving as president of the Emily Dickinson International Society, we convened our worldwide membership meeting at Asilomar, and met at Jewell Park in the morning fog for a White Dress/White Suit parade through Pacific Grove. In early morning fog, residents showed up with dogs on leashes to contribute to the enactment of Emily Dickinson's poem, "I started early, took my dog, and visited the sea." From Japan and Australia and Ireland and Paris, and all over the U.S., people engaged with Pacific Grove with awe at such a city where poetry is part of governance and its providence.

Now, despite everything that communities face these days in terms of demands, crises, and needs, a city where poetry matters carry out the letter and spirit of Whitney Lechich's vision of her legacy gift of a perch for poetry. The publication of this book by a Lighthouse Avenue denizen is an example of the commitment to poetry in everyday civic life that animates what citizens can do to bring us together around the campfire of poetry, this ancient practice. In these pandemic times where hugs are lethal, and smiles are masked, poetry is a way of speaking and listening and caring. I continue to serve and be nurtured by this community in which the consciousness of poetry in its life is still green, in the present imperfect.

—September 11, 2020

Preface

I

The Wisdom of Ramona (aka "The Pest), Age Four

Oh, earth! Do we ever really see you? This question was hammered home to me. Literally.

It is a glorious May morning in Helsinki as we stroll along the harbor. Blue and white flags flap and sway and snap in the breeze, orange tents shade trays of gleaming gold and orange fish and gold and orange potatoes and crimson and gold berries, wooden boats swash up white water, gulls sing, white tulips and golden daffodils adorn the bursting-green birch-tree covered hill. It is Wordsworth, it is Milton, it is Herrick, and I am Corinna, going a-Maying.

I don't see it coming—it smacks me on top of my head. Or rather, I smack it. A sign in the middle of the sidewalk, propped up on poles like a goalpost, warning Danger! Heads up! Look out! in three languages. I walk right into it—right through it, slamming the top of my head into the bottom edge of the sign. It is stunning. I'm staggering, piteously clutching my head, wailing, ohh, ohhh!

I am in so much pain, but not so much that I briefly say thanks my children aren't here to be embarrassed.

The next few hours I am propped against the curb with a hastily improvised bag of ice on my head brought to me from the ferry bar, freezing water dripping down my neck. A good look.

The joke is on me—yes, it is pretty comic (if you aren't me and even if you are). For years I, like you, have been an apostle of the philosophy, "be present in the moment," "be present in the world." (I know you ascribe to this philosophy—after all, here you are reading a poetry book.) The idea of being present is ancient, global, and trendy (e.g., Diaz's *Lead by Morning: 365 Days of the Present Principle*).

However, this was a case of not walking the talk.

How it was that I could be walking down the sidewalk on a sunny morning in Helsinki and walk right into a sign, a sign warning of danger ahead (a-head! Ha! Ha!) is beyond me. But it illustrates my theme here in this book. It is good to look where you are going. It is wise to see where you are.

For the past years I have swished a romantic mantle of identity bestowed upon me, the opportunity to serve as "Poet in Residence" for an enlightened community, the city of Pacific Grove. We might expect something so evolved as a poet having a civic role in a city calling itself after an ocean named for peace and a grove, a time-honored word for a stand of trees, a form of forest in which ancestors around the world gathered to ponder our being. From Plato's ancient grove of olive trees dating back to the bronze age (3300 BC), to William Cullen Bryant in "A Forest Hymn" — "The groves were God's first temples"— groves are conceived as sacred places of consciousness. Groves have so much power just as words that today high-end shopping centers and residential communities are given this name to impart a cultural lustre for cognoscenti. Pacific Grove was founded in the spirit of learning, where religious groups and the Chautauqua movement led retreats in a tent community to slow down from the world and focus on what matters most in living this life.

It makes sense that a poet in this ethos, living near Lovers Point (named for a religious practitioner), would leave her Victorian "tent" house to the city for the use of poetry. Whitney

Latham Lechich made a legacy with her clapboard Poet's Perch, a gift to Pacific Grove. Its mayor and city council audition and vote on an official city poet, and I found myself—pinch me!— with this title. This present.

II

Genius Loci

Question: can an old plump limping lady cover outdoorsman Thoreau, seeing Walden woods in Pacific Grove, its fields, sidewalks, and beach trails, its placid pond in Robinson Jefferish thrashing seas?

This book is a chronicle of both a particular and universal experience: being a "poet in residence."

What does that mean, exactly—being in residence? Of course, we're in residence, we all are. But perhaps we're not always conscious in the way that Thornton Wilder means, in his sorrowful scolding us in *Our Town*, or that Thoreau means when he says he went to the woods because he wants to live deliberately. It came to me, living in our Poet's Perch on 18th Street, made as much available to me, a citizen of our city allowed to rent it, as Thoreau's cabin at Walden was made available to him by Emerson, a city father. Emerson said to Thoreau, go, create ... be.

And so said the City of Pacific Grove. My job: to live consciously, aware of what it means to dwell in a city about the same size as Walden Woods, the property Thoreau walked every day—and yes, he walked to the town less than two miles away, to go to the post office and have some lunch and maybe meet up with his mom. His Walden was very Pacific Grove. My P.O. was a two-minute walk. My pond (aka Pacific Ocean) was a three-minute walk.

In the 1892 "Victorian tent" inscribed on the front cement

stairs with *Whitney Latham Lechich*—the poet whose legacy was this house, left to the city in the cause of poetry— and a plaque bearing the name *Nancy Davis*, to honor the mother of the man who first built the house, a house as wide as Mary Martin circling her arms in the opening scene of "Sound of Music," I lived as modestly as Thoreau in his cabin. I stored our family furniture, everything except my piano, desk, dining table, and ironing board —and books. My piano served as a bookcase; the kitchen counters were also my bookcase. The dining table was my bookcase. There was a desk, but it was also a bookcase. The ironing board was a bookcase.

Within sound of barking seals, and gulls, wind and waves, passersby neighborly talking on the way to get coffee (you could hear everything), rumors of cougars just sighted, complaints about cars left on the street, I felt I had my finger on the pulse. Here was a chance to go not "to the woods" exactly, but to a Grove, a Grove of Academe conceived as a learning community, to live deliberately, to practice the self-conscious art of being present, to not take for granted what is there to see.

I wanted to do justice to this opportunity to see if in this hurried scattering world of ours, I could actually be a poet *in residence.*

So, I began to pay attention to what it means to be in residence. *Genius loci* is an ancient concept, a spirit of place: *genius loci* defined as a protector of place, a sensibility with a sense of responsibility to and for a place, and perhaps what comes with the title Poet in Residence and the place itself, Poet's Perch, is responsibility to this place in how one writes about it. The way we characterize something leads to a new sense of how to think about it. In a sense, how we see each other, and our earth is a matter of life and death: trash or treasure? What is of value? What is worth preserving? When I read poetry, I am roused to care about things I didn't even know before how to spell, things so inconsequential, so vast becoming cosmic pals, becoming mystery before my eyes—and I know that's what is at stake in how we treat each other and cherish existence: seeing the world as if seeing itself could save it.

My purpose, to do justice to the opportunity to be in place, to honor this title that wriggled and writhed with a life of its own, a poet, in residence. How? Awake, in the way Thoreau urged ... a way of being conscious in the morning. The day is cracked open like an egg, darkness broken up to reveal color and shape, and unleash sounds of excitement. Every morning is extraordinary. It's a new beginning. A quest for morning, then, a guest of morning. I love that the ancients thought of writing about place as *genius*, that genius has something to do with how we are aware of place. That casts us all in the role of genius, the word itself containing I, you, and us together. We have to be here. Be. Here.

I have been a cheerleader for the consciousness that is brought about by "slowing down" with poetry, reading and writing it. I have felt responsible in what I write and teach and preach to do justice to the gift of consciousness for living on earth. I love how Pablo Neruda titles a poetry collection *Resident on Earth, Residencia en la tierra*. He was fiercely and intensely aware, both as a social conscience and as a lover. To read his odes on salt and lemons, tuna and potatoes, is to feel and taste earth's natural and unnatural history, its horrors and exquisite joys. I have wanted to be conscious, to be a resident on earth, in the way described in e.e. cummings' concluding couplet to his sonnet "i thank You God for most this amazing,"

> now the ears of my ears are awake and
>
> now the eyes of my eyes are opened.

I realized that one of the ways I feel *in residence* is reading poets who invoke a greater consciousness of being. I have been an English professor for almost fifty years, and founder and host of a weekly hour radio show on poetry, *The Poetry Slow Down* (broadcast from Sand City first as KRXA 540AM, then radiomonterey.com, and now podcast as BarbaraMossberg. com)—its theme is slowing down "to make the morning last," as Paul Simon sang. I thought about how poets make us conscious of residing in a place—Frost, or Emily Dickinson, or Mary Oliver in New England, or Jack Gilbert, and Linda Gregg, in Greece, or Wordsworth in the Lake District, or Gerard Manley Hopkins in British fen and glen—Scott Sanders, Wendell Berry, and all today's "eco writers"—how Proust said, "when I went to Venice I found that my dream had become, incredibly but quite simply, my address."

How to live up to our address, with gratitude and wonder. Looking with wonder makes our place a wonderland. To be conscious when we walk down the street—to see where you are (I learned this lesson the hard way) is a way to make good on the promise of the day, to be glad and rejoice in it (Psalm 118:24), to make the morning last and save the day—and ourselves, when, as Thoreau said, we are *awake*.

But he despaired that we are mostly *not* awake in our waking hours—he says he wrote Walden like a rooster's crowing. The title page included an epigraph: "I do not propose to write an ode to dejection, but to brag as lustily as Chanticleer in the morning, standing on his roost, if only to wake my neighbors up."

T.S. Eliot in *the Four Quartets* said, "we had the experience, but missed the meaning." How can we live and experience and not know what it means? Thoreau was proactive in his life, trying to ward off the tragedy of dying only to realize he hadn't lived at all. It was altogether possible, from his point of view, that we could miss the meaning, but what a comic predicament of being human! Doesn't this express the paradox of our lives? Yet if somehow, we can slow down our hurtling and stressed lives, the raw data of experience comes into focus. Some kind of Keats' *Truth and Beauty* emerges.

This book is how trying to be present slowed me down, even stopped me, in the act of trying to express with words, meditations chronicling my experience seeing and not seeing and trying to see, which made every place I went a terrain and tumult of consciousness—a Walden, a Grove, to invoke as hallowed terra incognita. I *considered the lilies*, and monarchs, *splendor in the grass*, neighborly civics, the Poetry Collective, the parades, the sidewalks and festivals and celebrations, the High School poetry flash mob, the hardware store, the Grove market, all part of the consciousness. I addressed my address.

In one project, I applied to the Oregon State University Trillium Project bringing poets and scientists together, where I applied the concept of being in residence to staying overnight at Shotpouch Creek in the Andrews Experimental Forest as a Walden, me a would-be Thoreau in search of morning moments. In another, I wrote about returning to Helsinki, Finland, a place I spent two years in residence, trying to capture the land and light in words, to get it right, and in another, to Yosemite, where I lecture in the summers for the Sierra Club's headquarters in the Park, the LeConte Memorial Lodge (now Yosemite Conservation Heritage Center), and in another, to our family home in Pasadena, all to me a way of genius loci, being in the grove, in the groove, feeling groovy, making the morning last.

From Poet's Perch, all the books piled high on my piano began to sing self-consciously notes by minds *in residence*. I found myself writing poetry about writing poetry conscious of place, wherever I was. I would read the newspaper and find poetry in those pages about our community. I would sit on a park bench, or on a log under a tree, or in a parking lot (at "The Grove"), or on my chair at the Poet's Perch itself, and slow down to explore that moment, right then and there.

II

A Grammar of the Present Imperfect

You are thinking, yah, yah, pretty noble, but—with all due respect—HOW DID YOU SAY YOU HIT YOUR HEAD AGAIN? (just asking)

Exactly: (I forgive you—it is totally deserved) There I am, slouched on the sidewalk with melting ice on my head, soaking my snappy suit worn for my university lecture on Neruda and Whitman and Thoreau and Emily Dickinson and all those icon poets in residence, because I didn't notice the writing on the wall, as it were. So to speak. So perhaps my message here is a grammar of the *present imperfect*, to try to honor the spirit of what the poets say, not what I *do*, not what any of us do ....

So! The title "Here for the Present" speaks to this concept of responsibility, the least we can do, in response to our senses, what we are given to live on this earth: what we mean by being *here.* The actual words of the title are from a fellow resident on the Peninsula, Beverly Cleary, from *Ramona the Pest.* It's the long awaited first day of school for Ramona (age four), and she has just met her teacher:

> "I am so glad you have come to kindergarten." Then she took Ramona by the hand and led her to one of the little tables and chairs. "Sit here for the present," she said with a smile.
>
> A present! thought Ramona and knew at once she was going to like Miss Binney.
>
> ... As she watched her mother walk out the door, Ramona decided school was going to be even better than she had hoped. Nobody had told her she was going to get a present the very first day. What kind of present could it be, she wondered, trying to remember if Beezus had ever been given a present by her teacher.
>
> Ramona listened carefully while Miss Binney showed Howie to a table, but all her teacher said was, "Howie, I would like you to sit here." Well! thought Ramona. Not everyone is going to get a present so Miss Binney must like me best. Ramona watched and listened as the other boys and girls arrived, but Miss Binney did not tell anyone else he was going to get a present if he sat in a certain chair. Ramona wondered if her present would be wrapped in fancy paper and tied with a ribbon like a birthday present. She hoped so.
>
> ... "Don't you want to learn to play Gray Duck, Ramona?" Miss Binney asked.
>
> Ramona nodded. "Yes, but I can't."
>
> "Why not?" asked Miss Binney.

"I can't leave my seat," said Ramona.

When Miss Binney looked blank, she added, "Because of the present."

"What present?" Miss Binney seemed so genuinely puzzled that Ramona became uneasy. The teacher sat down in the little chair next to Ramona's, and said, "Tell me why you can't play Gray Duck."

Ramona squirmed, worn out with waiting. She had an uneasy feeling that something had gone wrong someplace. "I want to play Gray Duck, but you—" she stopped, feeling that she might be about to say the wrong thing.

"But I what?" asked Miss Binney.

"Well ... uh ... you said if I sat here, I would get a present," said Ramona at last, "but you didn't say how long I had to sit here." If Miss Binney had looked puzzled before, she now looked baffled. "Ramona, I don't understand—" she began.

"Yes, you did," said Ramona, nodding.

"You told me to sit here for the present, and I have been sitting here ever since school started and you haven't given me a present." Miss Binney's face turned red and she looked so embarrassed that Ramona felt completely confused. Teachers were not supposed to look that way.

Miss Binney spoke gently. "Ramona, I'm afraid we've had a misunderstanding." Ramona was blunt. "You mean I don't get a present?"

"I'm afraid not," admitted Miss Binney.

"You see 'for the present' means for now. I

meant that I wanted you to sit here for now, because later I may have the children sit at different desks."

"Oh." Ramona was so disappointed she had nothing to say. Words were so puzzling.

Four-year-old Ramona has her finger on the pulse. I think her misunderstanding being "here for the present" points to something essential about the seeming multiplicity of the word "present." To be present, in the way we mean consciousness, to be fully alive, awake, aware, is a present to oneself.

But being "here for the present" also speaks to the way our time here, our own life on earth, is temporary. We are living here for the time being. For the time, being. We have to *be* in a more conscious way! Seize the day! Carpe diem!

I know. Who am I to say—to find myself, an advocate of presence, "doing justice to the gift of consciousness in this world," weeping in public, clutching my head, wondering if blood streams down my scalp? I have not walked the talk.

The ironies are delicious. The lesson, not a metaphor, not an allegory, but literal. Watch where you're going. If you saw the sign I hit, you would think there was no possible way for anyone to not see it and clunk their head. Ah, ah, as I re-clump the bag of dripping ice on my head, thinking of Emily coming back down to earth after she's died in Thornton Wilder's *Our Town*. She is reliving a moment from her childhood, and sees now that no one's really aware of each other, no one's in the moment:

Let's really look at one another! It goes so fast. We don't have time to look at one another. I didn't realize. So, all that was going on and we never noticed... Wait! One more look. Good-bye, Good-bye world. Good-bye, Grover's Corners ... Mama and Papa. Good-bye to clocks ticking ... and Mama's sunflowers. And food and coffee. And new ironed dresses and hot baths ... and sleeping and waking up. Oh, earth, you are too wonderful for anybody to realize you. Do any human beings ever realize life while they live it—every, every minute?

Wilder's narrator, the Stage Manager, answers her:
The saints and the poets. They do some."

She returns to heaven:
Yes, now you know. Now you know! That's what it was to be alive. To move about in a cloud of ignorance; to go up and down trampling on the feelings of those...of those about you. To spend and waste time as though you had a million years. To be always at the mercy of one self-centered passion, or another. Now you know — that's the happy existence you wanted to go back to. Ignorance and blindness."

So as I strive *to be* in residence (a lot of the time but obviously not all), to honor the news of us, to try not to lose the moment in obliviousness, I know I lose the moments constantly. It all goes so fast. I don't know if it is possible to capture aliveness alive, make morning last, but we can try to try. A whack, a smack, is a good wake-up call to be here for the present. *Here* is what we say, when we are present, accounted for, count me in, and *here* is what we say, when we give a present— here is something for you, with thanks and profound gratitude. *Here*—when you read these words, saying how I was here for the present, thankful. It is not forever. I know this. Sort of. But it seems like the grammatical term, "present perfect"—the perfect Blake knew when he said, "kiss the joy as it flies"—It's going to fly. Perhaps the joy is that it flies. In a vibrational universe nothing stays put—not even the dead. But glory be! —here we are, on this common ground, right now. It seems right.

Here is to being "in residence" together with you! Here!

Barbara Mossberg
Poet's Perch, May 2, 2014, and September 25, 2020

A Good Look: Ice Bag Beret with Water Dripping Down My Face.
Photo by Christer Mossberg

Part One

The Sun Rose—and other everyday curious happenings

Warming up writing sketches of amateur in residence contending with sky, mirror, and other breaking news

Peninsula Loomings

Kiss the joy as it flies, William Blake

Deus ex machina is not going to happen. That sudden whoosh, upsweep when the cardboard train bears down and I'm suddenly born aloft in a rescue engine of reprieve and flight. To fly above the stage— I yearned to be cast as the *Wizard of Oz* witch and do my cackly aaheh heh then shriek *my little pritteee* (gleeful snarl *you and your pesky little dog*). But I am too much. Hefty, embarrassed by the tumult of being heaved and cranked by pulleys. Yet sometimes I feel a hoist, so lifted it is alarming. Yes, the headache that grounds me, but I'm making green tea, morning has spilled sun all over this cottage, it is messy with light. For some reason, for no good reason, I am feeling too good, a quiver from inside out. It feels slightly dangerous to feel so well. I had not planned anything special with this day, I am in faded lifeguard shorts and T-shirt, writing, and not going anywhere. I rise to make more tea and it should not feel this good to be alive, Paul Bunyan enough to feel this planetary heave within me, interior lakes where my boots fall, witch enough for brew and glee, Monet enough to paint the day the water lilies in my core, William O. Douglas enough to do justice to this spacy conviction of sky, of tree—the pine outside the window in the wind, how it is to me just now, enough: I stand Bunyan, swoop with my witch's broom, my breath is Monet's brush, I am of Douglas' opinion: let the trees decide. Maybe not feeling so well because there is the headache and backache so maybe it is happiness. This whatever it is. And I'm *kissing the joy as it flies*, you can't put it down, you have it give it to somebody, a ceremony. Some cause to celebrate, a you:

so I'm here mishandling happiness and maybe feeling good
or not and wondering if I am up to this size of being, a little
intimidated at the largess of epic life, this whatever I can give
you, and so I go back to my chair and write these lines, not epic,
but some internal *Iliad* is about to happen, some myth breaking
free of tragedy right in me, and I hear wings beating, I tremble,
already more than mortal, and ready, when gods consort with
us—making a mess of day—the holy chaos in a glimpse of pine
against a western September sky— looming.

Day Break: Take This

I'll tell you how the sun rose—Emily Dickinson

Dawn, my mind says, a poet's word, as suddenly the dark room startles, becomes not light but visible shapes, and in a window a bright orange glow breaks the dark—"it is the East"—my Juliet is light, no need for metaphor. I grab my phone to take this scene but it is not charged— so my eyes have to be my *camera*, my dark room, developing it, recording it. Not able to be a photographer, reduced to age-old words, I go outside in the cool morning air, trying to see the way a camera sees, so I can tell you how the sun rose.

Isn't this who we are—in the face of something momentous, we "take it" to show someone.

And so this is my photograph of dawn.

As if it could be *taken*.

Whatever breaks darkness, the self that cannot bear to see such sight alone—the grey horizon, the turquoise space above the dark line, the orange stripe, pink and orange and white blotches of sky, red glow, orange.

We throw these words for color at the dark. I realize the camera cannot take the cool morning Pacific Grove air   that you breathe in, the chill of your skin, or the sound of the gulls, or the emptiness of silent streets, shop windows still dark.

The camera cannot capture me, limping along, the camera cannot capture me, my happiness,writing to you, from the dark room of my heart, camera obscura, my sense of gift of being out in the morning to see the sun rise through your eyes, to tell you this.

Pacific Grove January 21, 2014, 6:14 am

A gull's cry just now:
pulse, pulse.
What do you have to say, gull?
Are you speaking to me?
If so, what is my answer?
Now more rapidly, *pulse, pulse.*
We know what cries mean.
Ah, ah, ah.
Working the muscles of morning air.
Is this your CPR?
And a train whistle. Whoooo, a long exhale.
Something wants me alive.
I almost can hear the waves down the street,
their splash and crash. Their sighs.
The sound breaks silence apart into breath of busy bodies.
Every body's business on earth.
To live in a place where I can hear the sounds moving earth
lungs
Back and forth, back and forth, swoosh, woosh.
Tide speak.
Moon voice. Heaves.
The pulse of PG inside and out, swoosh, whoosh, creak,
    squeak,
Splash, crash, woof, ahoooooo, its heart throb.
This poem is my answer, gull.
And my question.
Back to you.

I'll Tell You How the Sun Set

The allure of a stunning sunset Tuesday led to a woman spending a cold night in a half-submerged boat in chilly Monterey Bay waters. The 45-year-old woman, who took a motorized dinghy from the Monterey wharf area to watch the sunset from an open-water perch, was rescued after being spotted by a fishing boat about 9:20 a.m. Wednesday." ... Her condition was "well for being out there for approximately 15 hours in very cold water and cold air," Stanley said. No one had reported the woman missing, Stanley said. Her name was not released. The rubberized dinghy started to lose air, then the motor fell off, then it got dark and a fog swept in over the water. The woman shot off a few flares during the night, but no one saw them probably because of the thick fog, Stanley said. The half-submerged boat apparently drifted throughout the night. But details of the woman's ordeal were a little fuzzy because of her hypothermia, Stanley said. The fishing boat that spotted her was just passing by the area, and its crew alerted the Coast Guard.—Monterey Herald

Earhart and Mead's deal. But my conscience could not override my kick in the Fall annual luncheon meeting, at which little ladies with blue hair wearing hat and gloves stood and reported on their summer. Holding her purse against her knit sweater, one would say, in a quavering voice, Well, I was in Cairo, so I went over to Nepal to do the trek with Annie, we took the new North Ridge route, and we worked on the Sherpa school project and Ethel's Library Committee was so helpful, and then we went on the submarine under the Pole with the Uger Expedition, I am transcribing my notes for the National Geographic Special for my interview next week, and on the way back I visited my sister Martha in Tulsa and we went out to lunch.

Me, I would be sitting there thinking, and you are thinking now, what was I doing there? It seems I was a groupie of people who have been somewhere and tell us about it. Even though she said I'm Nobody and never left her bedroom, Emily Dickinson told us how the sun rose (a ribbon at a time). John Muir told us how it was to lie nights in the summer Sierra. My heroes. So, when the Society of Women Geographers met at Florida's Sanibel Island, I flew.

Arriving at night, explorers checking in, no one knew I was not an explorer. I had a chance. I thought of all the explorers. I left my luggage in my room and went out outside—*alone*. What would John Muir do, I thought. Explorers are never afraid. So, I went into the darkness—no one knew. I was Joyce's artist as a young woman, *alone and free and near to the wild heart of life*. I felt my way in the total darkness through shrubs to the beach—led by the sound of waves. I had no idea where I was, what was here. This is what they do, I said. Arriving at a spot of sand, I lay down on my back and was Muir, to *behold the canopy of stars*.

I was so the adventurer. I lay alone on this strange beach and was part of the universe, Rumi's *bowl of light*. Yes, my skin was tingling, but I thought it was the cool sand, excited heart. I decided to not worry about patrol jeeps running me over, berserk men blanketing me, because I was an adventurer. I was a reporter on the scene, to tell what the world was up to that you can only know when you are alone in the wilderness.

The next day when he arrived my husband said what happened to you? I was laid up on the bed, swollen to twice my size with welts from no-see-um bites. The conference went on without me, all the reports from space and exotica earth. I had no idea what they would say in their reports of being out there.

But when I read about the woman who wanted to see the sun set off Pacific Grove Lovers Point and set out all by herself, I got it. *No one had reported the woman missing, Stanley said.* Oh, she was so proud of herself. To rent a boat! Out in the ocean! A motor! This was epic! Odysseus! No one knew she was here. This was hers. She was in this dinghy all alone, the old woman and the sea, a mile out, on this glorious expedition, and everything happened the way it always did for seafarers, the raft was losing air, and the motor fell off, she was adrift, carried out by the currents, and she figured out how to use the flares—yes, she!—pink in the white fog, and no one heard her cries, and it became dark, and when they found her fifteen hours later, slumped in the half submerged craft, "details were a little fuzzy because of her hypothermia." So, what she was going to tell us about the sunset we do not know. After all. But why she went—I can tell you all about it.

The Grove Market, My Neighbor

It is early morning. Too early. My daughter who cannot eat gluten is hungry, and I have set out in the most ancient of ways, to forage something for my child to eat. Nothing is open, everything is closed. I walk to the Grove Market, to see when it opens. 8 am, over an hour away. The lights are on. I look inside, and I remember my first-grade class where we learned "store" and this store is like that: a soft lighting, bins of arranged vegetables, wood floors, an old-fashioned feel, where you do not feel lost among rows of towers. You feel just right, the size you are. Your life seems orderly and possible.

Behind the deli counter, people in white aprons are smiling. They are slicing tomatoes and working at tables, and they look happy. I take in the scene, and although the store is closed, I am happy, looking at the happiness inside. A man comes to the door: he does not say, "We're closed." He says, like in a fairy tale, "Come in, for whatever you came for." He unlocks the door. In surprise and gratitude, I walk into the aroma of things baking, a morning kitchen, the way your house would smell right now, if our families were as they were, the way we used to live, before we lost ourselves, in urban aisles of the world that make us feel puny, when neighbors were there and their doors were never closed to you. In a world that often seems like for whatever it is you want, nothing is open, everything is closed, now you feel a citizen of an old world, buying eggs and butter in a market with a kind heart and jolly goodness. In a good world, it is never too early.

Poet in Residence

I sit by the window, dotted with rain,
As leaves slap the glass in the wind.
Two people walk by, holding umbrellas,
And I am grateful for the view, a Monet,
A Manet, making 18th Street in Pacific Grove,
A hop or hobble from Lover's Lane,
A Paris street in the spring—
Art is the only place it is quite so wet.

Oh thank you, for choosing a purple umbrella,
Oh thank you for your choice of plaid in this day,
And the plain black, its dignity,
The shape of a world seen from stars, or sun in eclipse,

Its solar flares, and the luminous grey, the luscious wet,
The waving tremors of the leaves in wind,
On such a day, how uncomplicated life is.

I sit in our Victorian tent of 1892 where Whitney wrote,
And gave to our city for a Poet in Residence,
And this morning, I am thinking of what it means
To be a poet in residence,
On our earth, in our noble towns,
Among all that grows and was formed so long ago.

The marvel of it, of what it means
To sit beside a window on a rainy morning,
A witness to earth happening before my eyes—
A bird flies upwards just now—
Black flutter zigzag while white gull flaps across grey roof—
Bliss happening in my ears, quiet clapping,
A brook-side sound of water lapping,
A hiss of car wheel,
a deep-throated laugh under the umbrella floating by.

I'm Shaking It I'm Making It But the Woman in the Mirror Doesn't Move at All

Sometimes the woman in the mirror is not you. That's how this poem will end, I'm telling you right now. I don't want you to worry, we all need to relax.

I go to the gym like I always do, to use the treadmill. There is a class going on called Zumba. I'm not the exercise class type. I had just eaten, ok, I have to back us up a bit here, it was yesterday, my friend tells me about this restaurant on Forest where the owners are so nice, and people need to encourage them to stay in business, and the wife works so hard making pies and making cakes too. So to the rescue, wouldn't you? I call my good friend, when we go out, we each order a different dessert and then order a third to split since we can't decide on only two. That one. I say we have to help out here. She agrees. We are both supposed to be on a diet. I eat chicken adobo with rice, pizza with anchovies, and a berry pie with ice cream, and a Tuxedo cake, about six inches high. And there is some left over which I take home, and eat for lunch standing up at the sink, which seems less momentous as an eating act than sitting at a table. I gobble it.

And that is why I found myself in a class called Zumba, although I should have known, I should have known better. You are already saying, what were you thinking, and worried how this will end. Even though I told you not to worry. But now you can't believe what I say. You are shaking your head. Who could be so—well, frankly, so recklessly ignorant? I face a lady in tights with—I look around, I'm the only one who is plump, I realize they are a dance team, and they begin to hop up and down in crazy zigzags of the hips, so many angles going here and there. I am trying to make each and all of these motions, my arms thrust high, my knees are bending, my hips are swirling, my rear is extending, I am gyrating, I am hopping, I am spinning, I am twisting, I am leaping, I am hoofing it, I am stomping it, I am marching it, I am shaking it, I am working it out. The sweat is spouting from me. I am panting.

And then I see this woman in the mirror, she is wearing my clothes, what I wore to the gym, but she barely moves her legs. She is a stiff mannequin, some stately robotic queen, bending a bit at the waist and extending her arm graciously, in slow motion, to bid me be on my way. Meanwhile I of course am a whirlwind, you would say that if you saw me, a ballerina gone berserk on Latin music, I am cavorting like a harlequin, I am a windmill. That woman in the mirror is not me.

And maybe this is who was with me on the treadmill. I was not holding on, so there was no way for the machine to monitor my heart rate. And yet the machine texts me, Do not hold on to handles, and then it tells me my heart rate, as if I am holding on, and I realize, someone is with me, someone is holding on. That is the woman in the mirror, perhaps, who wears my clothes, but she is not me, I am a member of the dance troupe, not the dignified calm lady who slowly turns, lifts an arm in some kind of farewell salute, and leaves. Don't worry: I am not she. Sometimes the woman in the mirror is not you.

After a Meeting of the Pacific Grove
City Poetry Committee

A hat on the sideboard, I cannot say *was left*, or *sits*, or lays, because those words are not right for what that hat is doing. It has taken over, you could say it has taken a leadership role in my dining room, all right, a *coup d'état*. Without lifting a finger, it owns the furniture, the room is no longer the room I have lived in. Everything belongs to the hat.

Maybe the room was always rebellious, always had it in it, to conjure this hat, brimmed for chin up escapades, bedecked with wide sash ribbon cascades. *Bedecked*, you heard me say, it's *beribboned*, *festooned*, you see what I'm saying, having to use these words which don't belong to me or my life, these words it brings to the table now which needs quiche and good cheese. Its graceful pluck transforms the room to a Monet scene, the walls become French doors, windows open to a terrace where a woman stands in white flowing dress with pink sash, or is this England, haberdash, London outside, The Street Where I Live, Freddy singing, or is the streetlamp in Paris, my bedroom a Renoir boudoir, am I blushing, where is my corset? My life is become a *je ne sais quoi*, a bustle, a hustle, a rustle, there's parrots and lace and panache, words I have to think now, say now, ways I have to live now. Oh, I could return the hat, I could see it as a loan, and give it back, but the truth is, you know the truth is, the horse has left the barn.

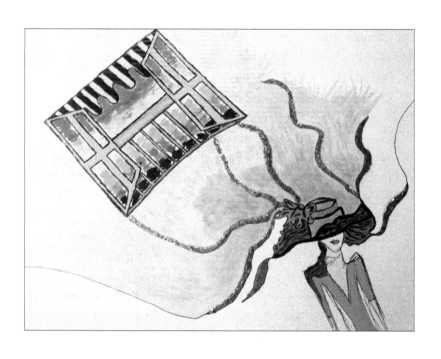

Part Two
FIELD WORK

In which I aspire to walk like a Camel,
or however morning is supposed to come
walking a mile in Thoreau's shoes

The Trillium Project: In Search of Morning

I went to the woods because I wished to live deliberately,
and not to find at the end of my life that I had not lived at all.
—Henry David Thoreau, *Walden*

... spreading wide my narrow hands/to gather Paradise
—Emily Dickinson
. . . without which men die miserably every day
—William Carlos Williams
. . . tongues in trees, sermons in stones,
books in the running brooks, and good in everything
—Shakespeare, *As You Like It*

Thoreau was perhaps the first official Poet in Residence, of Walden Pond, in the Walden Woods, outside of Concord, Massachusetts. He delivered a public report, Walden, including "Where I Lived and What I Lived For." He accounted for the time he spent. In this spirit as Poet in Residence for Pacific Grove, I submitted an official report on my project for Oregon State University (OSU) chronicling how I spent time alone, going to the woods deliberately, to encounter Thoreau's version of Morning.

Disclosure. I'm the least Thoreau-ish wilderness type you can imagine. You think I'm being modest, because that's how you are, generous, forgiving, the grace of overlooking, but it's probably a good thing you can't see me. I'm a plump lady whose age is 64 although I feel 14, except for the limp—what is that about? One thing is clear: we were never meant to see ourselves, from the outside in. We were born only to see others, to see this universe, from inside out.

I go into my deepest roots for courage and nurture to find a new way of time in our world, through presence in wilderness, using Thoreau as my lens. Suddenly, William "Bill" Stafford appears as a presence. He has inspired so many others. If I am entering the chasms of darkness, a Dante-ish Inferno, where wild animals snarl in my path, and I quake in fear, it appears that Stafford is to be my Virgil on this journey. The epic poets have my back.

On my way from Pacific Grove, CA, driving up to the Andrews Experimental Forest to the Shotpouch Creek cabin where I will stay, my Eugene, Oregon, friends hear about this project. They tell me about a dear friend's funeral service they attended for James Russell Sedell, who was connected with this Oregon State University program bringing scientists and poets and artists and philosophers together. That is my dream! They gave me a copy of Sedell's funeral service program.

While staying at Shotpouch Creek Cabin, I reflect on the program of the service, realizing that the man who was associated with this place and poet's center felt that William Stafford was critical to his own creative life. As a scientist and community leader and activist, he constantly quoted Stafford's poetry, to the extent that Stafford was considered inextricable from Sedell's own life. Two of Stafford's poems were read and printed out as part of Sedell's funeral service.

I am inspired to make my own creation of the meaning of this project of finding Morning in my life's Day with the reading of William Stafford's poetry. Stafford is an alive, morning, happening presence in our lives, perhaps "the thread" we are holding. Reading his poetry is like a sermon structure, a poem as the day's "text" from which to spring into reflection on the day's news (I like to show off a little by saying "Bill" on my radio show, the special pleasure to have known him). I read Stafford's poem as a call; I write a poem in response.

My official work here in my Trillium Project as Poet in
Residence is to find morning—what Thoreau meant by morning,
revealed to him when he went to the woods. I am here in the
woods, dutifully, full of faith, to discover the ways of morning.

From "The Trillium Report" by Dr. Barbara Mossberg to OSU/Creekside Project at Andrews Experimental Forest

Morning Hour
This is good to reflect on, right now, on the simple life, here
at creekside. The funny thing is that it takes so much work
to be simple, to unknow, to come to knowing. The grace of
bafflement. To understand what a thing it is to live a life, here
on earth, we have to somehow bring ourselves back to our
original way of knowing earth, when we knew nothing, nothing
but soil and tree and sky and creek, and of course that was
everything.

Morning Minute
Deciding to forget the howl I heard, I walk outside on the
grass to the edge of the little meadow overlooking the creek.
It is messy with branches and rocks and trees. It is muddy. Its
sound is delicious. Its sound is like the texture of berry pie.
It has seeds in it and is brambly, its voice. I love creeks. The
only thing you can do is love them. You can't swim in them
really or go in boats or float or sit there and watch them the
way I do ponds and lakes and rivers with herons taking off
and landing and ducks gliding and diving. A creek is jumpy
with light, splashing over rocks, trees bend over it, everything
is in it, what flies and crawls and swims and hops and leaps
and gulps. It makes the best sound of all. I stand, listening and
watching it, amazed that I am standing and doing nothing but

standing and listening and watching and being amazed. And then I realize that I am breathing in, that the fragrance of the creek and of the trees and grass and flowers is intense flowery woodsy and I realize that I have no language for any of this. I don't know the words for the smells and the sounds and the sights of what is here.

Morning Minute

If I wait quietly, I will not interrupt the sun right now, settling on the leaves on the tops of the trees like an orange furred animal.

If I do not move the wind will shake the trees and make them shiver.

But if I begin to sing, just now, who knows what will happen,

Maybe I am one more bird or maybe what was howling will join me.

Would that be wonderful.

I am the least howling person.

Or maybe the howl I heard was me.

Or could be me.

If I stop writing and stop thinking, I will not interrupt what is happening right now.

What is happening right now will happen to me too.

Morning Hour

Now I am on earth, as people always were on earth, as evening appears in a purple veil. There is a quickening in the air. It is the moon which has made a creek's ripple in the currents of the night. Do you know the way the moon hangs in the sky, even though we are told it is really circling our earth, which we are told really is round, even though we are standing on it and

although arced it is flat, that is how I see me, and your spirit—
sometimes I am a slice, sometimes whole, sometimes behind a
cloud, a quiver, and your spirit is this earth I circle round, and
we are bound to each other, as this apple tree here is bound
not only to this grassy field right here but to the space between
the branches where the sky lives, where its birds bring back
whatever is in nests that makes birds fly.

Morning Hour
In memory of James Russell Sedell

The poems he loved, Bill Stafford's "The Way It Is,"
The poem about the thread, the thing you hold
No matter what happens, what tragedies and how we age,
"while you hold it you can't get lost."
"The Well Rising," about the spring on the hillside,
The swallow heart, "thunderous examples. I place my feet/
With care in such a world." And Raymond Carver's Late
Fragment,
Which goes, "And did you get what you wanted from this life,
even so?
I did.
And what did you want?
To call myself beloved, to feel myself
Beloved on the Earth." In his service, celebrated by people
Who have blessed this place by the creek, people said in
unison,
"He leads me beside still waters;/He restores my soul."
Those voices are here tonite, rejoicing in a mind
That wanted woods and water and fish and flight
For us every hour of our lives, all the days of our lives,

And that loved poetry and poets because in them,
Has always been, woods and water and fish and flight,
That kind of joy along with smoked oysters and Pinot Noir
Earth has up her sleeves, for you her beloved.

Morning Hour
You can explain it however you want, but the stars
Are lessons in wonder. All we have to do is wonder
And we've got it right.

Morning Hour
First, I am taking notes on the program for James Russelll
Sedell,
With wife (Ellen), friend of Chuck and Doris Burkland (at
Willamette together).
July 5, 1944-August 18, 2012.
A man who showed up with a bag of smoked oysters and Pinot
Noir and Triscuits, who in the middle of jogging on a camping
trip at the coast, comes across store and gets wine and jogs
back with it to camp.
Chuck tells me he always shows up with a bag of groceries
(high end for frolicking) ready for a good time. It seems he
lived all his days. He found out in a July he had pancreatic
cancer and died weeks later. He encouraged his wife to buy
the house they had been looking at, in Lake Oswego, and she
did, next door, living next door to where they lived, almost
a mirror image of their life, their house, without him. Three
children. She loves to solve puzzles, work on taxes.
When they told me about him, a scientist who loves to get
people together to celebrate life with poetry it seemed he was
a person at the root of the OSU program. His funeral service

pamphlet identifies him as possibly connected:
The James R. Sedell Fish Conservation Fellowship Program at OSU through National Fish and Wildlife Foundation, contact Kystyna Wolniakowski.

Long-Term Ecological Reflections Program at the HJ Andrews Foundation through OSU

Fred Swanson

The people who spoke at his service were:
John Dennis
Fred Swanson
Heather Chase Alexander
Gordon Reeves
Michael Weinberg
Dennis Hanson
Kelly Burnett
(children Ted and Jennifer)
Stan Gregory

Tree planting led by Mike Furniss and Rick Zinn
The poems were poems he often read aloud:
William Stafford,

The Way It Is

There's a thread you follow. It goes among
Things that change. But it doesn't change.
People wonder about what you are pursuing.
You have to explain about the thread.

But it is hard for others to see.
While you hold it, you can't get lost.
Tragedies happen; people get hurt
Or die; and you suffer and get old.
Nothing you can do can stop time's unfolding.
You don't ever let go of the thread.

I think about this poem. At first, he's following the thread but then he's holding it, as if it is a lifeline. Something very slight and fragile and yet it is enough, a lifeline he never lets go of. What is this thread. This one thing that leads him safely through changes and catastrophe and fears, that he always has. That no one else can see and that he feels he has to explain, or try to explain. Is it his faith, or his idea of life, that in spite of everything, "time's unfolding," —is that image that time has us originally curled up, furled, folded exquisitely perhaps like some kind of seed, or flower, and then petal by petal we unfurl, some design, to become ourselves, glorious, on the way to unraveling, spread so open and far and taking in sun and drying and freezing and fading and falling and becoming detached and then reattached to ground, loam, soil, earth itself from which we came, its flesh and spirit. Is that what he means by time's unfolding, of our lives. And we can't stop it, but/and we don't ever let go of the thread, our understanding of the continuity, the mind that relishes and savors and absorbs and holds fast to this life. Like a fish swimming, it seems, against the current, holding its own—that fish follows, holds to this invisible thread that keeps us on track, that protects us from the pain and the flood, the washing out, of what happens, as we truck on, as we proceed.

What is your thread, your idea of life that keeps you intact? That survives and helps you survive what happens, the loss and confusion and sadness and sorrow and dismay, the guilt that we can't change what happens to the people we love, their dismantling.

That is why I love that this poem is paired with the 23rd Psalm, that sees the dismantling, the unfolding, the sagging, as something also protected, for a greater enduring life beyond the flesh. This Psalm is greatly complex. It starts out with the Lord out there, talking to us about this Lord and his relation to him, the Lord as his protector, like this thread. Then he addresses the Lord directly, saying "thou." He is speaking to the Lord. Then he again is speaking to us, assuring us and him(her) self, *surely*, isn't that a lovely word, a word of reason and hope fused (there is grace of some acknowledgement of doubt in it), surely, goodness and mercy shall follow me all the days of my life; and I shall dwell in the house of the Lord forever. So, who is it to him. It is to himself, and the way in our prayers perhaps we are speaking to ourselves and our Lord, reflecting, hoping, affirming our relationship and our faith, going back and forth in a consciousness of togetherness, in conversation, and reflection.

The Well Rising

The well rising without sound
The spring on a hillside,
The plowshare brimming through deep ground
Everywhere in the field—

The well rising without sound
The sharp swallows in their swerve
Flaring and hesitating
Hunting for the final curve

Coming closer and closer—

> The swallow heart from wing beat to wing beat
> Counseling decision, decision.
> Thunderous examples. I place my feet
> With care in such a world.

Now this poem: I found myself loving how he managed to rhyme *swerve* and curve, his poet mind working these images of sound and the absence of sound. I can hear the creek as I write this. A well rising without sound—what does that mean? The well spring of water ... brimming up out of earth, everywhere— then in the sky, swallows, also silent in their own ways ... and as momentous ... for what earth contains? This liveliness? And at first talking about the absence of sound, then, the heartbeat of a swallow "thunderous examples"—the loudest possible enormous sounds. So the most silent, the slightest, most delicate of movements, of rising and swooping, are momentous, huge huge earth sounds of power. So when he says he places his feet with care in *such a world*, what is he saying about this world? In such a world water rises out of earth, silently, swallows make arcs. Is he placing his feet with care out of fear for himself, or out of a protective feeling? Or a feeling of awe, of reverence? Like when we step into a cathedral or into a grove of trees and we find ourselves quieted, quiet, stilled, still, some kind of appropriate slowing down with respect to honor wonder.

And what is this swallow heart counseling, decision, decision. The thunderous examples, loud, noisy, shaking, earth-shaking, quakingly fearsome, glorious, immense, powerful, coming out of universe's way of being and speaking. Water rising silently, evidence of spring, a spring, well nourished, swallows angling for the "final curve" coming closer and closer to—what? Is it the curve of the earth? What are they after? In all their arcing darts and bursts, hesitating and swooping suddenly, making the decision to go for it? Is it the exquisite timing of life that knows what to do and how to do it? When he is careful about placing his feet, is it a consciousness of how precious is such a world, that contains such things as wings and sweet plentiful water? What is his decision? Is it to go carefully? Reverently?

These two poems meant very much to Jim Sedell and he quoted them and recited them. They were perhaps his ethics, his own mission and values statement, his anthems of being a naturalist in our world, sharing the good news of nature, and finding that poetry was a way to do it. It gives me great joy to know that Raymond Carver's poem was also significant in this album of his psyche, in his backpack of spirit:

Raymond Carver
Late Fragment

And did you get what you wanted from this life, even so?
I did.
And what did you want?
To call myself beloved, to feel myself
Beloved on the Earth.

Then a Unison Reading:

Psalm 23

The Lord is my shepherd, I shall not want;
He makes me lie down in green pastures.

He leads me beside still waters;
He restores my soul.

He leads me in paths of righteousness
For his name sake.
Even though I walk through
The valley of the shadow of death,
I fear no evil;
For thou are with me;
Thy rod and thy staff,
They comfort me.

Thou preparest a table before me
In the presence of my enemies;
Thou anointest my head with oil,
My cup overflows.
Surely goodness and mercy shall follow me
All the days of my life;
And I shall dwell in the house of
The Lord forever.

Morning Hour
Now it is day, and I am drinking coffee with ice, making of my inner streams perhaps the quickening of earth's creeks from glacial run-off, from mountains, that knowledge of enduring.

Morning Hour
I photograph a flower growing amid the profusion of unknown wild plant life, grasses and shrubs and plants and trees, what's what so unknown by me, and this was one of

the definitions of "wild"—profusion, confusion. I think of the efforts of people to grow flowers and care for our earth, as it is "their own." Cultivating. At our human best. Working together with earth to grow and be grown. The message of the Little Prince, caring for one flower, his rose. I remember how Thoreau wrote about his beans and cultivating them, how it was not just beans he was growing and working so hard at, toiling in the soil. How perhaps—whatever we are given is our rose, our beans, including the thorns and toxins and stooping and aching and sweat, that goes with caring for them. That whatever we care for also nourishes and gives a joy that is seen in every aspect of how we live our life, this knowledge in you of how and why to care for what is given to us. In that way whatever we have is our rose bush including its thorns and toxins and sweet tough orange tree, or trillium not stopped by clear cutting, defiant and forgiving among stumps, its message of resilience of spring, surprising lilac by the road by Spring Creek, that requires perhaps just our notice, our gratitude.

Morning

I am called here. I have so much to learn. Who called me? Who called the trillium? My journey with Spring Creek is begun. There is more day to dawn. The sun is but a morning star. I will return and be alive again today, this day, this time, this hour beloved.

To be continued. The horse has left the barn. This is not news about the barn. It is about the horse. Our story lets go of that barn. That is not our story after all. Our story is the horse. The trillium.

Part Three
THE PLEIN AIR MIND

Triumph: Returning to Helsinki
For Markku

tri·umph [trahy-*uh*-mf, -uhmf]

noun

1. the act, fact, or condition of being victorious or triumphant; victory; conquest.

2. a significant success or noteworthy achievement; instance or occasion of victory.

3. exultation resulting from victory; joy over success.

4. *Roman History.* the ceremonial entrance into Rome of a victorious commander with his army, spoils of war, and captives, authorized by the senate in honor of an important military or naval victory. 2).

5. a public pageant, spectacle, or the like.

I Yksi

What explains why we love a place?
The high-rock cliffs by the road;
Birches line the way,
The sinappi-colored buildings standing at attention—
Daffodil bouquets—
A triumph into town.
So good to see you,
Solemn, so seriously beautiful,
Even in cold rain.

Totta kai

II Kaksi

These birch trees
Immediately as we turn out of the airport—
Birch trees! The exotic and precious at your front door—
Look out! I want to say, be careful, do you know how rare you are,
How rare this is? Just how you are?

The rocks—the rocks—
The bark both white and black,
Red and grey and brown—pine and birch—just turning Spring
Here, yes—even in rain you sing—

Totta kai

III Kolme

I'm so excited coming to Finland,
I eat what's served on the plane—
I'm not hungry—
I don't even like white bread or digest red peppers,
But I eat it.
Already so close, the only answer's yes.
To everything.
Long ago I surrendered to you, Finland,
The moose has left the barn—
I trust whatever is given—
It started when a man named Markku said believe me,

It will be good.
And it was good.

Totta kai

IV Nelia

Unsmiling
You bask in my gaze like a Finn—
Unruffled, accepting your due,
Bursting with green, out of winter you've just been through.

Totta kai.

V   Viisi

It's a mutual love—
Neither of us has changed—
(If you haven't neither have I—)
You're the same, I exclaim,
And it's not just an answer to a prayer,
It kind of is the prayer.
It is the prayer.

Totta kai.

VI Kuusi

This long procession into town,

My heart takes it all in,
Approving everything I see,
To come here feels triumphant.

Helsinki, you don't think I'm old.

Totta kai.

VI *Kuusi* (Because you can never say kuusi enough)

I wouldn't miss this for the world, of course.
The world a young man once told me is centered right here—
I believed him. It is the world
In which I return to my senses.

It's just a road into town from an airport, they might say.
Yet to breathe such air as you, to see each tree of you, you
Rocks, you, buildings along the way, it's Helsinki! What does
That mean, after all these years?
How can I explain heart's return, a triumph, as I utter joyous
Exclamation, *safe!*
Simply and mysteriously, I'm coming into home.

Totta kai.

Finnish Journal: On Being in a Place

July, and so begins the end of my struggle to capture Finland in words. How I have tried, how every day, looking at the mustard—the tubed "senappi"—rounding buildings, seeing the plum evening sky, the towers silhouetted against the half moon rising fast last night, gold, then pink, then white, in a purple not-night soft satin sky, glossy yet matted.

I have tried to think how to translate what I see into words. Every day is research for my poem that will unlock the sparkling blinding glass door. I stare. I watch how light manifests itself. I think of how to express what it means, this land of light, that neither photographer nor writer can capture.

Finland is here, I guess, because, like the Finnish language, like the Finns, no one can capture it. It is untranslatable. It cannot be transformed. Words break against it, brittle, limp, and meanwhile the cobblestones absorb light and in Fall rains glisten, radiate, and the land is never ever dark, never without light.

Finland is the earth's top of its head, patted by sun. It is the closest thing to living on a star, and I can't explain why, can't tell why it is different from any other place.

One becomes silent, first in contemplation, and then the silence, the pauses, of the Finns, make sense. In this silence is the knowledge of what is there but can't be said.

It is a language about language, a way to speak what doesn't need to be said, perhaps the unspeakable, in words. The only language is the language of light itself, its voice a whisper or shout, angry or depressed or ecstatic, hoarse or mute with joy. It is a language I have tried to learn, but it cannot be spoken, only read, only heard.

These words, then, are the words of struggle and defeat. They become whatever you capture, cannot be captured, and you are left forlorn and foolish with only the empty trap you set and your need, your wish to take it home and have it forever. So, I leave, with the wish intact, and these words, empty traps, because—I let it go, alive, whatever Finland is to me, and thus always to be there for me, outside and beyond these lines, outside the range of voice.

Washing the Lake

I'll wash the dishes, I say.
Nothing more than politeness—
It's my hands—I can't stand to get them wet.
But my hosts don't understand.
Then it turns out there is no dishwasher.
There is a lake.
I am handed a bucket,
And pointed in the direction of the dock.
Now, washing the dishes,
It is wonderful
Before I realize it,
Before I even think it is a poem.
Not the poem that comes to me,
But the poem I need to write,
The poem I wait for, do not even seek,
Ready as when you reach for the camera
When you see a certain scene,
To capture something you already know,
Or more—our guide, keeping us alive
In terrain we thought we knew.
It shows us how to know what we know.

Standing in twilight, a lake of light,
The two-fold wrinkled light of day and night,
Sky's shiny flabby folds,
My hands and wrists in rust-colored lake water and suds,
Sauna-warmed, feeling glasses slippery as eels

Skid from my tremulous touch,
Tracing their rims and sides as smooth as ice,
As ripe melon when you are scooping out the seeds.

I look at the lake.
I think, it is the lake whose edges I am tracing, its contours,
Insides, bottoms and sides:
Suds and ripples in the sunlight, they are one,
And my hands feel reeds and birches, clouds and frogs.

A poem is not the record but to explore. It is the map we end
Up with, yes, but the poem is also the reason for the journey,
Why we ever took off from what we know.
We think we do not know enough; we become restless,
We give up a known world.
The poem is our interpreter,
Telling us what we have seen.

The surface I see is not flat,
Neither is it broken with reeds. No, it resembles more—
Something insubstantial, like clouds appear, no, sky,
Something that isn't even there, not even to see.

It's the light now, it makes the water seem opaque,
Shimmer but not ripple or break,
Like the definition of matter. Nothing solid about it,
Nothing could float on it, it isn't even there.

I am staring so hard, but the problem is that there

Is nothing to see but reflection, as lake appears nothing
But sky. Trying to find words for what I see,
But the words don't come. This is like—what, I wonder.
Poems need analogies.
But what I see does not need anything.

Lily pads dot the surface. We say that.
Really, they define the surface. Patches of light like steps,
Like cobblestones. The clouds, so white and expressive,
Define the Finnish blue—
Well, what is the verb for what clouds do?

This landscape defeats me,
When I try to understand it in words.
A lake at twilight, but not just a lake.
Washing dishes, as if I am washing the lake itself.

Never mind the poem.
I am enjoying washing the dishes right here and now.
Sometimes just the facts are enough. More than enough.
I am washing dishes, and I think, this is significant.
This matters.

Washing the dishes outside here is a restoring of order,
Sensuous exploring of surface, finding shimmer,
Shimmer of glitter and shine and suds.
My hands emerge with fork or cup. How many women
Have stood here so, by some lake or river or sea,
Scrubbing the bowl that held porridge? This is Egypt.

This is Maine, this is history, this is Truth and Beauty.
I dip my fingers in cold lake water. I am happy.
I take my time.

I am sorry when the dishes are dripping and clean,
spread out on the table--bowls, plates and cups,
Glasses and spoons. Of all the things they hold,
This is what I want most,
My hands in them, on them, in water.

After a Sauna I Find Myself
Sans Clothes, Sans Skin, Sans Breath,
Sans Need for Anything
But This and Not Even These Words,
Not Wet Like Fish Aren't Wet

In no way will I do this.
But I take off my shoes
And make my way to the smokehouse by the lake.
This is going to require shedding a lot for me,
And my feet are the first to absorb
The prickly lessons you learn when you strip:
Ants, rocks, pine needles and dirt.
I hop and try not to call attention to myself.
I might as well be a harlequin among the pines.
The clothes come off, dropped on the porch.
That's how I think of them,
"t h e   c l o t h e s ." They are not mine.
I don't know them anymore.
They are so far away, so inaccessible, so suddenly unhelpful,
Lying like that, not even dead,
Just immaterial.
How could they leave me like this?
It's not that I renounce them for their betrayal,
Going like that, gravity helped.
But these lumps on the planks,
These can't be what goes for me.
Me? Not Me.
I stand without them.

They are a clown's clothes,
A heap of patterns on the planks.
They can't be what I go for,
My shell, what holds me, my identity.
A balloon with the air let out, crumpled wrinkles, that's all.
They are like the puddle of the witch in Wizard *of* Oz,
Her remains after getting wet.
No witch left, so what is this?
Whatever is left, was before, will be.
Abbreviated me.
Now I'm truly on my own, and being alone is complex and whole.
Suddenly—there is just oneself.
What I hide, what I dress,
What doesn't belong to the world,
Is all there is. I don't think,
I don't have any clothes on.
I feel complete.
This is all, this is enough.
Not thinking, *I don't have any clothes on,*
Only skin and wonder,
I enter the smoke hut.
I bake.
I am batter, becoming something. More, or less.
Eyes tearing in smoke.
Water on the coals, goose bumps rise. Am I burning or frozen?
Bend over, they say,
I bend over, my wet chest on my knees, my eyes are closed.
My skin has lost whatever it knew.
It doesn't know what it knows.

It doesn't know how to know it.
Or it is no longer what it was.
I don't know why I'm wet,
Can't tell what is leaving or entering,
What is mine or in the air
Settling like insects on my far away skin:
I am a place,
An intersection, no, a process, and it's going on right now.
Body, steam, lake,
Sweat, tears, vapor,
It's all the same,
In the sauna,
You know it,
How everything is water: how we belong to this earth.
Immersion is redundant.
I hear the splash.
So, I must be in.
What I hear must be me.
For moments there are no words. I am stopped.
I am over.
I am some form of primitive being. No bones, no spine, no lungs.
I am beginning. I am the original.
There is nothing to put on.
After a while it is not cold.
I plunge my face again.
Breasts float by somewhere near, like lily pad blooms,
Or aspen leaves, catching the light, white, white,
Legs, arms, are golden under the water,
In the sun-drenched lake so green, so brown, so cold.

Heat and cold, water and air:
It's how things are begun,
Universes, earths, us, now.
It's not cold, I say,
And I kick my legs, watching the spray form litala glass.
I lie on my back and look up from my bed.
This is where I live. This is who I am.
The blue sky, the white clouds, are a Marimekko blanket over me,
And I toss and turn, aware of fresh flesh, floating and warm,
Free of bones, free like lily pads or aspen leaves or ripples
Only rooted or controlled
In the sense of the profoundest tie to this nature,
Connected to it by my certainty
That now I live.
We know these things as a fish knows light,
Or worm, ground.
I lose myself as I shiver on the dock.
In the sunlight, the water makes me shine.
I am not even thinking of these words.

Book Me, Sir: John Muir Takes a Sauna
with the Naked Ladies of Kuopio

Who lying on Finland's boulders doubts rocks are breasts,
have hearts beating within? The pink warm glossy rocks of
Finland, its luxuriant flesh, pink largess glorious speckled pink
flesh glistening, oh God of largeness, moose or granite. God of
pulsing heart. White wispy steam rises from the lakes, from the
cloudberry bogs, from the ladies, from the fire, from boulder
shoulders. This is prehistoric, dinosaurs are going to appear any
minute. *Treed*, knees up, on a ledge in the dark log cabin, flesh
all about, the wiry lean Scot is huge with ecstasy, he is tickled
pink, he is a deep deep pink. Flesh all about, fresh flesh smoking,
steaming, quivering, baking, sighing and heaving like an earth
amaking.

At first, he's making mental notes to build himself a sauna
for his place off the Ahwahnee meadow by the Merced, a glacial
place where the dinosaurs also rubbed their backs and left
glistening scales. Then he is distracted, thinking of creation and
glory. The large ladies surround him, and he is heating up. His
blood will burst. Now, to the lake, a pink parade, they leap. Not
heart-stopping cold as the Merced, but as gold, gold under the
surface. And then the silver light of the storm coming up over
the trees fiercely, the purple prose of the thunder as he climbs
white now out of black water, following the ladies he thinks of
the expression, *to be moved*, of the expression, *it was a moving
experience*, he thinks of how trees do it, not just the limbs and the
leaves, which anyone can see, and which he knows because he
visits trees and stays overnight, too overcome to leave, but the
trunks, he knows they step carefully and magically as elephants.

He is naked, wet and streaming, the wind is fresh with him.
Trembling, he enters the dark steaming hut smell of birch and
smoke, and in the half light, the pink flesh, the pink shoulders

of giants steam and stream and glisten and run, volcano, glacial run-off, he remembers how the earth was made, all molten, melting, how he would cling to these rocks, nest in their ledges, cling, cling, oh pink listening earth inside, oh tremendous, tremendous, now for the first time he sits thinking of himself without bark.

He is borne by the pink goddess ladies of Kuopio who carry him, lay him on the dock. He thinks he is clinging to a rock, he thinks it is alive, he lets go and is flying, trees dance and rocks breathe, space is alive as any river, he thinks he is a pink rock warmed by sun, he has lost track of who is alive and what moves and what isn't alive and what doesn't move what has bark and what has limbs and what has heart, but he knows that nothing is always there. So that must mean everything moves, something must move it, he thinks of what or who moves us. He is so little, but he is so ecstatic, his vision of glory is huge as El Capitan. Floating and cascading through the air, heart fall. He throws himself over the edge, onto the pink rocks rolling and grasping the soft moss, sweet lichens in the cracks, murmuring and rolling his eyes.

The ladies of Kuopio look on and approve. This man has gotten it right.

What We Bring Home

I stand by the window this last morning,
My bags finally packed (the glass, as if I could
Bring home the light on the water; the space
Just above the water where gulls gulp what shines
And glitters; the material, as if could wrap around me
The lumpy lime lichen on glossy smooth pink rocks;
The silky blue of the sky around scaly mustard building;
The spirits, as if you could inhale the smell of birch leaves
When the wind turns their green white; the gifts, as if
The gifts I bring home are the gifts Finland gives to me;
As if I can pack what I take out of a country).

I stare at what moves me, but cannot explain why
After all this time: the roofs from the eighth floor
Of my hotel, the green and grey peaks, spires, domes,
A circus of geometry where angles of soft color pierce
The sky, heart. The grey mottled sky, a batter of clouds
For some cosmic porridge—
O hearty, warm, nutritious Finnish morning!

The park below, bones of trees, brown bark, skinny limbs,
Brown slushy earth, dirty snow, the sludgy mush of ground . . .
My eye focuses suddenly on a tire swing, empty now
In March pale grey light.
I fill it in, with a child, and the world becomes technicolor:
Dandelions grow a foot high, I see stripes, hear children
Counting uksi, kaksi, viisi, kolme.

Again swirls our son, our hours in parks like these,
And I wonder, Finland, what you are.
Why this innocent bare landscape fills my heart,
As if this sludgy mush of ground,
Melted chocolate and vanilla ice cream spilled,
As if this landscape had put out tendrils to me
And they have taken root.
I am connected to this mud, to this skyline.

I pick up my bags, so full,
As if they could hold what I have to bring back,
As if you could pack your beart,
The breakable, the heavy.
I know I will ache.

Why are they not heavy?

I pick up this view of winter light and carry it.
Though bursting, what I hold will not break.
I carry whatever Finland is, and it is light,

It is light.

Part Four
PRESENCE OF MIND

Loafing and Inviting My Ease

It is only a reed—nothing to be seen,
This single stalk
Growing like a flagpole
Without a flag.
How it grows by the pond, free,
It could be a weed, wild,
Unplanted by human hand—
A random dart of green.
Then a dragonfly
Visits, sits on top—do dragonflies
Sit?—straddles it, rides the reed,
A translucent gauze, lace, with eyes.
And now I see the stalk.
And in my wonder at how precious—
No, beyond value, how much it means
To the fly, this moment of green in its life—
No, the simple green stroke, dash, with knuckles
Like some finger, simple and so singular,
To this winged creature
Is the world.

And to me, now, not the stalk of green,
Pencil-thin, with which I could write—
Not the winged intricacy
You can see through the color, the lace,
It's the togetherness of it, the cling,
How now it's a flagpole with a flag,

A flower with its bloom, complete,
A finished entity, a radiance; such grace—

I stand and marvel, how the dragonfly teaches me
What's here, what matters, what's still, what flutters.
My stalk heart now a bloom, at this sight—
How I'm taught, what's good if you're designed to fly,
This humble moment of green needing you,
Needing your visit to be seen for what it is,
A glorious thing, and you,
your needing of its plain being—

One home in pond's mud, one home in air,
This is where the meteor lands—
What I want to say is I'm seeing love
As how the universe works—
Dragonfly's kiss, reed's patience, a happiness,
One embrace.

The Improbability of Orange

You might ask me why I drive south four hundred miles to feed the fish. You already think you know and like to hear that it is because since my father's death I am trying to maintain his pond, the one he built with his own hands out of stones he collected and carried his whole life, the one he had blueprints for when he went into the hospital and emerged, I believed, to get this job done. And he did. He made a wooden sign (now faded), I Have Made This, planted by the pond, and what I know about filters and waterfall hydraulics and algae would fit into this line. I couldn't even open the fish food container, which was stuck, and even when I did and scattered flakes on the surface, there were no fish to be seen. The pond's water, so dark and murky. Perhaps they had died. And then it was cold, perhaps freezing in the night. And the raccoons. And the heron. And the neighbor cat. And the water evaporated in the afternoons. And then it overflowed, and a fish was floating. Now on my To Do list was pet store. Sure, he said. And I was given green fish in a bag. These aren't the right ones, I said. They are supposed to be orange. When they grow, the young man said. They have to establish the pond, he said. Whatever that meant! I would litter the surface with flakes, no fish in sight, and still I drove, and went out barefoot every morning, worried what I would find. Between the night's wild dangers and all I did not know—still stood and scattered flakes looking for signs of—and there they were, stripes of orange in the dark, green, water, the fish, who had survived the night, the frost, the quick paws. These darting moments of orange, arcs of orange, how did they become, how did they survive? Today I wake up and still undressed I hurry outside to behold a miracle, orange against dark and green, and this orange makes the dark water, the green water, what I love. In such darkness the pond was established, the orange so improbable in this world. The orange makes me love such a world, what can live in it. This is what I feed, this dark world, in all my incompetence, this is what I care for.

Why When Something Doesn't Work
Do We Call It a Lemon?

As the meringue bakes, air bubbles trapped inside the protein of
the egg whites will expand and swell. However, if the egg whites are
beaten too much, or if a tiny amount of fat is allowed to contaminate
the mixture, then the proteins will not be able to form the correct
molecular structure when cooked, and the meringue may collapse
when cooked. The meringue can be beaten into either soft or stiff
peaks. The temperature the pie is baked at and the method by which
sugar is added also determines the texture and durability of the
meringue.—1933 Cookbook

"but the fruit of the poor lemon is impossible to eat"("Lemon Tree")
—Will Holt, sung by Trini Lopez

I

At bitter life, you say, I will make a lemon meringue pie. This is
a blessing up your sleeve. I'm not saying that to say, I will make
a lemon meringue pie, is an easy thing. To say, even to yourself,
I will make a lemon meringue pie, is like saying, I will make a
Jaguar from scratch, and I don't mean the car. It is like saying, I
will compose an Ode to Joy. I will make a harp. I will re-wire the
house. I will apply the second law of thermodynamics to global
warming. These are things that can be done, with patience, love,
chemist's mind, geologist's vision, engineer's resourcefulness,
astrophysicist's tools. What I'm saying is, you can do this.

II

It's all about the spoon. Spoon against and with arc of pan.

Velocity, of spheres. Orb against orb, gravity, momentum, heat, transformation. Egg. You begin with the warm egg, cracking it open, and you end with revelation of egg, its insides. You are recreating embryo, life itself, what clucks and hurries and bustles and makes out of feathers and wrinkles a perfect package of life and life again. You are making something about resurrection, something ancient, and have you ever noticed, when a lemon tree lets fall a lemon, it is like a chicken hatching an egg, that perfect oval lying there, a gift of oneself, out of bark and soil and air, this perfect package of sweetness and pulp the taste of yellow sun.

III

Eggs the temperature of lemons on the tree. The same shapes. Think how the egg is lemon-colored on the inside, how egg and lemon are the same. Meant to be together, and what does this say about chickens? You don't know.

IV

You can buy crumbs, but you know they will not have the energy your smashing gives the crust, and it will lie passive, a beat-up humbled numb mass.

V

Try not to be afraid of the cornstarch, or at least know that everyone is terrified of cornstarch for how it will become curdles of gum or silly putty in your dish and there is nothing then you can do, except use it as grouting. But part of this dish is your belief that you can make lemon meringue pie unlike most people on earth including those who make it for stores using gelatin. It is no coincidence that lemon meringue pie came into being with the fields of chemistry if not also geology and astronomy. Right now, you are in the astronomical stage, galaxies are being born before your eyes. In just seconds, you yourself will be a force in which dust becomes glory, something miraculous that will become something complicated and whole and fresh and then, like a star, like all life, dissolve once again into the Universe. You are stirring and stirring this flour sugar salt cornstarch dust, trying to convince it they are all one and one for all, together at last, one coherent identity. And think of it, earth's soil and grasses and seas—grass, root, mineral—with the endosperm of the corn kernel, the amazing maize.

VI

You make zest a verb. Two lemons right into the frying pan—the flavor, right here, the vigor of the whole thing. Juice the lemons by hand, take pleasure in what cup you use to measure out the water—your favorite coffee mug, perhaps. Take pleasure in it all. Except after cracking the eggs: separating yolk and white, very difficult, at least for me—any yolk in the whites, they can't be whipped into meringue no matter what you do and you have to start completely over, asking whoever is home including your guests to go to the store and buy more eggs. Meanwhile use the wrecked egg mixture for your banana bread you already made when the day had legs with some whipping cream, vanilla, grated orange peel, bourbon, and golden raisins, for a bread pudding. You can also use it on your hair as a conditioner. With coffee.

VII

You now are ready for a glass of Moscato over ice. Hold in your left hand. Your spoon in your right, you stir and turn up the heat slowly (putting your Moscato down), slowly, slowly, stirring.

Nothing is happening, a white milky soup, but you keep circling, circling. You see some darker spots, like fish in a current you swirl. These are lemon pits, and you keep them in, how people know this pie is real. Tell people—whoever gets the most pits is lucky, says ancient myth. Tell them (a cook can make things, make things up) in many cultures whoever gets the most pits wins a prize, in ceremonies celebrating the river flooding at the full moon when everyone wears white and drapes the cows with orange silks. That the meringue symbolizes white of the moon, and the white milky soup the color of stars in birth. Soon you think you feel a little resistance as you slowly move your spoon around and around the pan, and you do—the mixture is congealing, and it is chemistry, you see that now, you have transformed solids into liquids and now some miraculous texture, and swiftly, now, swiftly, calmly, reach the bowl of egg yolks which you have beaten, oh, well, pour them over the mixture and keep slowly stirring the sudden yellow texture the filling, of lemon meringue pie— turn off the stove OFF and scrape the mixture into the crust NOW. Eat some-some Moscato will ease tongue burn, and it was tense there, but you did it, you did it. Who knew you could do it? I knew it. You had it in you all along.

VIII

You beat the whites. Yes, yolk got in. Your guests went to the store and bought more eggs, so started over. It's baking. The pie is like the view flying to Dublin and over Greenland, clouds or ice fields or glacier mountains, and flying, you think of lemon meringue pie, how your tree is doing and if it misses you and has laid on the ground a lemon offering and does not understand or worse if it worries when you do not pick it up. You imagine this alone lemon on the green grass under the tree, its gift, like an egg on the nest. You open the oven door: this is what you see from the sky, just like that. There, perfect, and you take it out, and you can't believe that it looks just like lemon meringue pie.

IX

You serve it warm. Hand out forks and say, dig in. You get the seed, and you know you were right, although you made it up: it is lucky, its slippery, bitter tang. This is always the case with making something sweet of bitterness. There is never any left.

What the Geranium Knows

A river. A bush. A person. An idea. A feeling.
Each is hard to perceive—what is happening –
And what causes the happeningness of it.
My computer just corrected me— the happening mess of it
And that is true too.
But the difference between mess and happiness—
I can't see it.

Your Inner Quiche Is Perfect:
Let's Focus on Getting the Crust as Good

I

The city poetry committee is on its way. Quiche is called for.
The first thing if you are serious about wanting quiche (and
sometimes we aren't, but it's the way Jerry Garcia reasoned about
his audience: people who like licorice. Not all people like licorice,
but the people who like licorice, like licorice). Only with quiche it
is also a case of timing—when you want it— it could be evening,
it could be morning, but the point is, you have to be serious about
the crust. The crust is the part to get right. Because frankly you
can't go wrong with the inner quiche. Whatever you put in, and
the possibilities are as never ending as a Texas road or Oklahoma
sky, or blue Pacific, or redwood you gaze up at like some Jack at
the Beanstalk, or story someone is telling you as you are falling
asleep, it will be just right. But the insides deserve a crust that
can be savored for itself, because that is the first and last thing
people will taste.

First, have you opened a chilled bottle of Moscato? That
is a good thing to do right off the bat. Let's drink a glass right
now while you read this.

The crust needs to be tasty in its own right. Otherwise,
why make quiche? We could make a pudding. That is not a bad
idea. A butterscotch bourbon pudding. You eat this under an
oak tree living when John Muir was still alive, before he broke
his heart over the damming of the Tuolumne River, around
a campfire, and it's cold and dense. You are wearing a heavy
cotton dress, striped, and a jean jacket. But a quiche needs a
crust that you put your fork into after you have finished your
piece and tamp it down to get those last crumbs. A person's

quiche plate after the quiche is eaten should be glossy as a leaf after rain, and that totally clean.

II

So here is a crust that I have made up but realize this is a metaphor of possibility in which you can dwell like Emily Dickinson. The point is, it has to taste wonderful. This crust I am describing is pretty good but you will come up with ways to make it great. There is a quick way that works, and a slower way. Choose the slower way with quiche. That's why we start off with a glass of Moscato. Take your time. Like lemon meringue pie, also a French invention, this is about s l o w i n g d o w n. It is about luxuriousness. It is about the most relaxed happiness. It would help if you read Jane Austin or *War and Peace* as you are making it. I also keep *Wind in the Willows* on hand.

All right. Let a cube of butter, unsalted or salted, soften naturally in a yellow ceramic bowl. Do not use metal. Yes, you could microwave the butter if you are in a hurry, but if you are in a hurry, never mind the quiche—heat up ready-made soup. I am not saying it does not work to microwave the butter, and I have done so many times, but the texture will go from a continent to sea marsh and become mudflats. Mix in some flour. I am using a gluten-free flour these days—millet, but any flour you choose is the right one for your quiche. Pour in a handful. Don't use a measuring cup unless you have a favorite mug with a rooster on it that was your grandmother's or that won your heart at the flea market for fifteen cents. This recipe is made the old-fashioned way, the way people cooked in days before measuring cups and metals and possibly shoes. If you wish, use your favorite coffee cup, but my way will save you an extra thing in the sink. Just pour from the bag. Now, some vegetable oil, a tilt, pour that directly from the jar, and some ice water, a wine glass full. Using a wine glass will give the water a sense of itself, a respect, that will be inspire the other ingredients. And some honey, you know how much, blackberry, blackberry honey, and spicy brown mustard, but any mustard is great, and use a lot—maybe what you think is a wine glass full? And perhaps some pepper. I sometimes use hot pepper oil too, a dash. And lavender. Today, we're also opening one of the jam jars you take home from the restaurant and never use, so I am finding Lilikoi, and I use that. You could finish up that orange marmalade you have when you are filled with nostalgia for your father and make hot sourdough rolls with butter one rainy morning with Rhine Wine, or pumpkin tangerine jam someone gave you for Christmas last year, that you have saved for the Big Occasion. Mix it up, put the batter in a pan with a spoon, smoothing it out over the surface of the pie pan and up the sides. It will fall down immediately because you don't have enough flour in it. I know I told you not to measure, but really, it's all right—do you really need it on the sides? I think you will be fine.

Did you turn on the oven? Did I forget to tell you? We were drinking Moscato and relaxed. It doesn't matter. Turn it on now to about 350. (You never have to have any other temperature. We are trying to get back to the days when an oven was a set of rocks and coals.) Sprinkle icy cold water on the top, and prick it with a fork, so that you are making tracks like a bird in the sand by the water. You want it to bake until the crust is browned and crisp on the edges.

You will have been breaking eggs and the fragrance will let you know that your crust is done. You take it out, and it is ready for whatever you have for it—eggs, cheeses, vegetables, seasonings, chicken stock, white wine, onions, and you sit down for a moment and work on a crossword puzzle. The kitchen is filled with the fragrance of crust made slowly. Never mind everything that is going on in this hurtling world. As for what you're going to put inside, you have everything you need. It will turn out all right. This also goes for the quiche.

III

Now you're going to have two cast iron frying pans. In one, you put half a stick of butter, some olive oil, and cane brown sugar. Heat it up gently and slowly, and then add some cut onions. Cut the onions any way you wish. I make mine half arcs because you want them a little meaty. They are going to be translucent, and sweet. They are going to be so delicious that you will want to eat them all by themselves. You should eat a few, with your wine, because that's part of what makes a quiche great, your own happiness in making it. By the time you are done, and people come, you are going to be too distracted anyway. So, enjoy it now. Those are just delicious onions. They cook so slowly. They slowly gurgle and turn brown around the edges, a little caramelized, but moist, and totally transparent. They will be limp. Let them relax.

In the other pan, you just put a package of pancetta, cubed, and start cooking it gently. After a few minutes when it is thinking about sizzling, add mushrooms. It works best if you begin with whole mushrooms and cut them in half or thirds or quarters in the pan, stabbing them randomly. You will want these in chunks, but they are going to be tender and full of flavor, with the caramelized pancetta, which is crispy, and then their meaty texture, to which you add the freshest pepper you have. This is going to taste so good, but don't burn your tongue.

Now you take your crust out of the oven. It should look like some desert geography you pass over in the plane, cracked just a bit, erosion, shiny on the surface. Immediately, add cubed cheese. Now here you have your pick. I like a smoked and smoky cheddar, and sometimes Jarlsberg, but it can be any flavorful firm cheese. I have never used Brie and it might be an interesting thing to try. But you don't want to overwhelm the taste of your mushrooms, which are tangy and salty with pancetta (you could use bacon here), and onions, which could be their own pie, out of some British nursery rhyme.

Layer on the mushrooms and then the onions, and let it sit. sit. Now, break the four eggs, or five, which should be room temperature, and whisk them as hard as you can. Now add heavy whipping cream—you can use half and half, but I like the texture to be more like a rich dense custard. I usually use too much, especially when I add chicken stock and the Moscato and it spills over and creates a big mess, and the proportions are all wrong. So, this time, err on the side of being a little ... little. Pour perhaps a cup of cream, and half a cup of wine, and half a cup of chicken stock. Now add shaved or grated fresh Parmesan cheese (any form you have will be fine), and some nutmeg. If you have mace, use a zester and get some of that top layer, which is nutmeg, but fresh. Add some freshly ground pepper, and pop it into the oven.

Now, bake it around 350. It should cook so slowly. After a while check on it and have a little more white wine. You could have used a Riesling, or any sweet white wine, a Rhine Wine. This is a time to set a table with a blue and white checked tablecloth, and a wicker basket ready for hot fresh sour dough rolls or some great bread you love, and olives the way my friend Carole makes them, with orange zest, and even if you just open a can, add the orange zest and a little olive oil and they will taste amazing.

The quiche is done when it looks a little brown around the edges and oozy on top. But the inside should be firm. That is why we cannot have it be too liquidy. We want it molten, custardy. The smooth, smooth feel of the egg and cream and wine mixture will contrast with the crisp pancetta, the perfect meatiness of the mushrooms, the sliminess of the sweet onions. Let it sit on the counter for at least half an hour. What? People are waiting. More wine all around. Bread and olives. Perhaps a green salad. Take your time. The quiche should be served a little more warm than room temperature.

The best thing is that tomorrow, when you wake up, you can heat up a piece in the microwave. Yes! It will be too hot and juicy and moist and is a wonderful way to start the day, and that makes sense, right? Because it's eggs and cream and bacon and onions, a biscuit-like crust, flavored with honey and mustard, which goes so well with ham and cheese. It is a perfect breakfast, but to eat it this way it has to sit overnight in the refrigerator and then be heated up (you can also use the oven, putting the piece in an aluminum pie pan, but in this case, the microwave makes the cheese melty).

You have whipping cream left, I hope. Good! That is for the pot de crème, with berries, and whipped cream on the side, and that is why in my list of ingredients I said a quart. You will be glad.

I Remember Being in the Now

One time.
It was a moment of happiness.
I remember.
It was in the mountains of Tennessee,
In a lodge room,
Where we met my brother and his family,
A rare time, finding each other in the middle of the country,
And we were sitting in the morning before checking out,
And we'd had breakfast—
I don't remember any of this.
We were checking out in an hour and it was that kind of time,
Between time, when nothing is expected
In this hour, of this hour,
There is nothing to do, nothing expected of me,
And we sat there, doing nothing, nothing but knowing we loved,
And were loved, andwere, just as we were,
And it was—can I say this?—
Perfect happiness—
How can that be? It was.
I was sitting on this leather couch, with huge beams overhead,
Morning light streaming through the window
A scent of Fall leaves,
And it was the people I love, and I felt that here, here, now,
If I died, right now, it would be okay.
I thought that.
I remember thinking that, this perfect moment of time.
And it was I guess because I was living in the now
That one moment.

Part Five

THE PERFECT IMPERFECT OF QUANTUM HAPPINESS

wild, n. uncivilized, undomesticated, not tamed or controlled

One day when I was sixty-four, I went down the street—on foot, at a limp, but wearing my stretchy black dress of days of yore—it was shorter now and came only halfway down my thighs, way above the burl of knee, it is sleeveless, yes, with my arms, orangutan, bat wings, and was going to do something about my hair. My hair, wild and no longer combable, tangled and fierce— my students said to me, Dr. B, I don't mean this wrong, but you are looking like a female Einstein, and the truth is my hair was very much like e = mc2, totally incompatible states of being on one scalp, as if you saw my head from space, continents covered with a cloud, breaks in it so you see the Sahara, grassy savannahs bordering dark forests, from a helicopter you see zebras running in a herd, elephants wallowing in a mud hole, lions in the golden grasses, red fox in orange morning sun, white owl in moonlight, the geography of a bird's neck, of a toad's forehead. To the salon lady on Green Street I said, please help me, make it coherent, but keep a little of the grey on top and two hours later, I am Newtonian, not natural but regular, walking down Oak Knoll, and my limp is now a lope, a gait, I am an antelope, on my way along the river, I am an Arroyo coyote, I am springing and sleek, camouflaged as the wild are.

Ode to My BCBG Holy Inappropriate Dress

First, the strophic dress TURN *Then me the antistrophe*
COUNTERTURN *Then you tell me.*

It was on sale. Shopping with my teen-aged daughter. MOM!
It's two layers, almost see-through. Beneath is flesh-colored
gauze—sewn into the bodice, and then flows free from the
neck and arm seams. That's it! That's what's going on with this
dress—Free. Flow. The top is bright soft red with white flowers.
It is so transparent, so skimpy, so flimsy: like a cloud manifests,
weightless, this dress flutters when I turn as if there is a breeze.
It has its own weather system, eddies of wind, currents, squalls as
I move, or even breathe. Even the sleeves, little flaps, bunched at
the shoulder, then draping down, fluted— the whole thing loose,
wavy, rippling, the V-neck gathered, edged with ripples. Ladies,
you know, help me out here. Then the empire waist, ruffles, that's
it: ruffles, all along my bodice, then, a ribbon sloping down into
a bow; material so light, so translucent, so fluttery, it rides my
curves lightly; and the dress descends, loosely, to a ten-inch
ruffle, bordered by more tiny ruffles. So you've got the dress,
and now you're thinking of me, what, am I four? Or, nine? Or
Audrey Hepburn at sixteen, or Maria from Sound of Music? I'm
dating myself here. I've turned sixty. So they say. My arms: you
know orangutans, the scope and heft of their feathered arms,
enormous, hang prodigiously. Now think of flesh: soft white
floppy, arms so heavy with soft flesh they dangle when I walk.
My breasts are hanging, too, filling nicely a 34-G, and they sway;
you've seen me and dismissed me as a comic turn in a thousand
films, the stout giggling aunt in the background, shaking to the
music. My belly sags and sways. My jowls, you see gravity at
work, erosion, fault lines exposed. Aging's geology.
    So now, you have me turning, now counterturning. Now the
epode.

Why? Why do I wear this dress? Well, isn't it obvious? I wore it in Rome, and the children rolled their eyes at one another, and gave advice on how to wear the bow, my husband shook his head without shaking it. I peed in the plaza (they fled)—Okay! It happens! But the stains came out nicely. And I wear it today, with pearls, to visit my mother, in her outpost in the assisted living place, where we have hired twenty-four seven care since her two falls and perhaps one stroke three weeks ago. She has not spoken since. Last night I lay my hand on her trembling hand. Together like that, they looked so similar—hers a little more wrinkly—a few more brown spots—red from coumadin bruising, my own hand in twenty-eight years—twenty-eight years which once seemed enormous—my mother of such size and heft to me, now a flutter in time—a ruffle, ripples on the surface, like stone dropped in pond, her ripples becoming my wrinkles, as pond absorbs our energy. Eighty-eight does not seem so far, and twenty-eight years a heartbeat, this morning at her bed with the rails we installed last week, so she doesn't fall out and hit her head—hospice, which she does not know about, or she does, and none of us knows, either, how something like this is read.

Is it clear to you this is my perkiest dress, so light it flutters when I walk—you would swear I was in the Carpenteria afternoon breeze; if it had any more ruffles I would fly; I am a flag of some weightless nation, like a cloud manifests. My arms are bare. I flutter, and flap, and sag. It is so light. It billows and sways and caresses each curve. I have plans for tonight—freedom and hope and time to finesse. I kiss her goodbye. She speaks: *you. look. pretty.* That's why. I wear this dress to face, face to face, heaviness, all gravity's laws, weighted with sorrow, and loss, and fear, in hospice, I bear it, I wear it, this buoyant excess, this innocence. Good style, good class: tell me it's an inappropriate dress.

Quantum Happiness at Charlie's Boathouse

In the soft blue bright hazy light
On a late summer day, late in the day,
Sitting on the swing at Charlie's Boathouse,
Is Margaret,
Blue Heron in residence.
OK, no one knows if she's a girl,
She's the one you can count on
To be there
On the days you are lucky.
You can't count on anything
And that's why we name, claim
Unclaimable facts about the universe
And pretend there is a science
In what we can see and when it is there
And what it means when we actually see it.

Our Margaret, she's standing, at first in profile
In the posture she posed for the bird-spotting book,
It's a hunched-over, dowager scrunched up look,
A little unkempt, too, sort of toad-like,
All bunched in the middle, then this head jutting out
Sort of peaky.
And then she unfolds from her crouch,
It's that sudden, and it is grace,
The long leaning extension of her neck peering out,
Ending in a beak resulting in a point,
A kind of Leaning Tower of Pisa look,

Sleekly balanced, geometrically angled,
Perfectly poised.
She stands, stands
While my heart takes in the scene
Like a child falling in a field of wildflowers,
Grasping them in fisted delight
At the capture of something so wonderful in the hands.
A picture you snap again and again
As you stay with it, your happiness
At seeing this sight, this sighting.
And then, before you know it,
You had nothing to do with it,
You were happy, you needed nothing more,
The bird lifts off, her feet folded back, flies before your eyes,
Her feet extended out as sleekly as her smooth neck,
One long line, defining sky, low across the water,
Flapping, her flaps against the perfectly still legs and body
Held aloft, no movable parts at all
In that long extension, perfectly engineered legs out straight,
As she so slowly, so balanced, gravity is not at work here,
Lands, and stands once again.

Well! I am beyond satisfied.
I see it, but how did it happen?
Sleight of Hand.

And then, no, another heron, flying perpendicular to the water,
Lands. And there comes another.
Now it is a new proposition altogether.

This is not any longer
The kind of wistful sense of heron as pet we get with a name,
Demystifying what always is so far away,
So improbable in our daily vision.
I was so grateful for one.
Now it is beyond the rules for what I need to see,
What I came for,
I am in way over my depth.
Now it is glory, and glory is always humbling,
Glory is multiple, numerous, a quantity.
Hovering on the edge of too much.
And then a white crane flies and lands,
Stands there in white long-necked peering perfection.
And another. And another.
There is nothing I can do with words
Now to do justice to this scene.
Art leaves. It is science.
I count, one, two, three, one
Two three, four,
Amazing quantity,
And what my mind is
Thinking is,
There are three blue
Herons,
There are three cranes, now five cranes.
Three standing, four flying, one flying, three standing,
Nothing adds up, it is all there at once.
The inaccuracy of the heart's computations,
Quantifying happiness.

Happiness is quantum.
The only thing I can do to state my state of thrill,
Enumerate a category of wonder,
Count as if a number says it all,
More than I can ever say.
Midas,
The king in the counting house
In the song of six pence.
When it gets right down to it,
Our great brains, our exquisite capacity
To recognize Truth and Beauty,
To compute wonder and behold,
Our complex minds of science and artistry
To comprehend, respond,
Are at square one:
One, two, three.
The beginning of intelligence,
Seeing pattern, this is like that,
They belong,
There are more than one,
They are different than everything else around them.
We differentiate.
We see.
All that's left is elementary, what we begin with,
One, two, three.
The engineered universe, laws of nature,
And all experience are
Facts
You can count.

Sitting on the wooden swing at Charlie's Boat House
As the sun goes about a leisurely plump orange setting
Down purples on soft blue hills
Like a parent gathers soft blanket around a child's shoulders.
Setting down soft purples and oranges on gray blue water
Rippled as feathers, sleek in places as neck stretched out taut,
Happiness is easy
And I can talk about it fine,
One, two, three, four, five.
Grateful, witness,
I count what never and always can be counted on,
Beyond any names, any words we could have for them,
Whenever they appear, just in time,
Summoned by our hopes we did not know we had,
By our need
For what is totally unexpected
But why we after all show up
In late afternoon late summer by a blue lake.

When I Think of You, I Remember
the Cranes in the Helsinki Zoo

For Mr. B

It was not the cold that took my breath away. It was seeing cranes jump and leap, a fluttery excitement that can't be expressed with feet on the ground; you have to bend your knees, crook your arms, shrug your shoulders, unfurl your great shoulders. They were undaunted in their joy, they were intent on dancing, such flapping happiness, my heart clapping.

Somewhere in our past you must have been Zeus—surely, I have seen this in your thighs—and I the maiden Leda, who took you trusting into my lap, stroking your soft neck, in love with you, beckoning you to me. And then you stood before me, unfurled, majestic in your wingspan, this was serious and powerful now, and I was on my own, in a new world.

We never hear what Leda thought, and I have never wondered until now. But the cranes dancing before us awakened my memory of that earlier time and that ancient and eternal life we shared, when you were both God and flew, in our Greek days by dry fragrant mountain valleys above the sea. And now I remember when you were the bird and I was your Nils, and you flew me over mountains and hills, through clouds, above shining winding rivers of white and pale green waters and jagged rocks.

And in the wingspan of the dancing crane, delicate pencil legs lifted to hop and skip, I remember happiness in your embrace; I think of the surprise in you, when you break out, sudden spring bouts of, bursts of, gestures of inexplicable and graceful moments, where you bravely stand and face me, and unfurl your wings, and, stately, lift your foot and begin to hop, and flap, for me.

These shoulders shelter me at night, draw me into them, warm and moist. I sleep under wings, under feathers, we nest. When someone would look at me it would look like I am lying, lying under your strong muscular wings; but when I think of you, and me, in your wings, I am flying, we are flying.

And once again, I am Leda, I am Nils, and my hair is in the blowing wind. It is wild, once again, how you like me, how you have always seen in me a wild heart, and you rise dancing and glorious, glorious and dancing, out of my dreams, as old as the hills.

Taking a Page from John Muir's Words
I Tried to Save a Willow Too Big to See

WOULD YOU CUT DOWN THIS TREE IF YOU SAW THIS WEATHERPROOFED SIGN ON IT ENCIRCLED BY A CHAIN MY FATHER WRAPPED AROUND ITS TRUNK?

What law or words could protect a tree? How could words make us see a living being in such a way as not to slay it? As being worth more than a flat lawn or tree-less view? What words could ground a law to hold such tree in reverence? The words I thought of did not serve. My father and I threw every rationale in the Book into this poem, beginning with the way that since Biblical times romantic poets like Wordsworth and botanists like John Muir have called us to gaze with reverence and awe ... this was our bald-faced strategy to save this tree when I sold our house in Vermont, and left it in the hands of fellow human beings. Every line was a call to see one's way to preserve the life of this tree. What did we leave out?

Behold!
The Good Luck Tree
Recipient of the John Muir Educator Society Award for
Promoting Love of Earth
A Vermont Treasure
Rare Magnificent Specimen Willow
This tree has inspired poetry
And dedication to the preservation of the earth.
All who live with this tree

Are protected by her strength; soil is bound
Preventing erosion and flood damage;
In life's storms she provides comfort and joy
And gives courage to the spirit.
Known also as "the Blessing Tree."
In hard times this tree
Awakened my wonder
And gratitude for living on this earth
And my commitment
To teach its beauty;
She has given me heart and seen me through;
Danced a hula, graceful as a ballerina in her tattered tutu;
As you come under her care, know
THIS TREE IS LOVED
And will love you too—

RIP Great Willow, 104 South Cove Road, Burlington, VT 05401

Night Hunger, Wild Hunger

The last thing my father says as I fold myself into a sleeping bag and he zips the stars leaving me to a canvas darkness darker than the night is what to do in case of a bear.

I sit back up, a letter about to spring free from its envelope. I have just flown five hours from Washington, D.C. Driven four hours from San Francisco in the Hertz car. Bought plums along the way, and Perrier with Lime at the Village Store. This is how I arrive at Nature. I'm wearing jeans and I'm ready to forget the worries in my linen life. I have worries. I do not lead a sensible life. A sensible life always has a cat in it, and a kitchen table to sit around. A garden to weed and a lawn to mow, and store to walk to. When you live a sensible life and drive, there are parking spaces. Your phone bills aren't higher than the heating bill. Twenty people plan your birthday party. They know each other. Your three children are there. When I call home, I have three calls to make each in a different area code. I have no place for bills, and I lose them. I run in the dark and the rain. Some days I only drink coffee. I risk my life in taxis. I work for the government, which does not respect me. I know what a sensible life is, I just do not live it.

And I have worries, the kind where you know you need a vacation: I have been using unacceptable language at cars that cut me off, shocking my son; mommies don't talk like that, he cries, he's six, what does he know? You're a poet, he says. I say, poets use strong language, but he's not buying this, he sees my wildness, along the Rock Creek Parkway shouting at drivers who can't hear me, at news shows about issues I can do nothing about, and I know that is no excuse, eternity will blame me for the potholes and homeless and lost generations of children and burnt land and reckless and ignorant cruelties, all cruelties are ignorance, and you knowing this is no excuse. I need a vacation, way, way beyond civilization, in car ad country. In nature, yes, but a national park, with my parents, greeting me, *Now Honey, no phones are going to ring, you can write all day, and no one's going to be mean to you.* (They know what the government is like.)

Now: bears. Yes, he says, the bears. They forage for food at night. They cause, and he pauses, quite a lot of trouble. Yes, I remember now, seeing trees with poems nailed to them, a stand of signs, but the yellow metal messages I thought I had time to read later are telegrams, Federal Law: Lock Up Your Food. Violators will have food confiscated and be subject to a fine. The rangers hold a meeting and advise: If a bear should approach, scare it away. Make an angry noise. Holler. Yell. Grunt. Bears understand this kind of language. They leave.

You get on a plane, praying in the taxi to survive the ride to the airport; you get as far away as you can get east to west, from civilization's complexity, to nature's symphonic order, and suddenly life is simple. You are scared of bears.

From my journal. *I didn't sleep well. Daddy said to make sure no food was in the tent for the bears—and if one came in, to yell, angrily—and I lay awake for hours, trying to think of what in the tent was edible to a hungry bear, and then the expression, hungry as a bear came to me, and I sat straight up, thinking of a wild bear's hunger, for marshmallows and cookies—-of his red eyes, of his claws, tearing at the tent, I thought of what would seem tasty to a bear—the cough medicine, the aspirin, the deodorant—Blue Grass!—the lotion on my lips—making a mental inventory of everything tasty about me— you never think of yourself as tasty—suddenly I realized I could be ... delicious—I was seized with a powerful sense of the bear's need—I held a pot in my left hand, and clutched a flat fork in my right, with which I was going to clang the pot when he appeared at the tent's zipper, snorting, wild-eyed with need of marshmallow. I held this pan and fork all night, listening for someone walking without shoes.*

The next morning, I am groggy and obsessed. Spilled

milk on the campsite's wooden table makes me tremble, my son spilling tuna out of his sandwich (don't you realize bears LOVE fish, I scream). He looks at me. I scan the camp with a bear's gleam, what's here for me? My mother tells me, *Darling* (in her New York accent), *You're not going to have an encounter with a bear, I assure you. You will be lucky to see a bear.* I examine the table next to the tent where we prepare our food. Triscuits: I practice LaMaze breathing to keep myself from passing out. Getting ready for bed, I ask Nicolino for a pot to bang. He brings me a cast-iron frying pan, drops it on my right elbow, the one I injured in Budapest in the taxicab last month, and I cry. He looks at me. My parents are bewildered, *we don't believe this!* I am thirty-nine. I turn thirty-nine as I cry.

It is night again, the time I have dreaded, when I must go to the tent. I inspect it again, to make sure, to make sure, nothing edible is there. I go through the suitcases, pulling out each T-shirt, sock, knowing it is crazy. In a pocket of my son's pants, I find a Gummy Bear. We are sleeping with Gummy Bears. I take out all the clothes, again, turning out all the pockets for what will lure this bear to my tent. His hunger, which makes him paw into windshields, cross meadows lit with white moonlight, shake RV's down, mangle for sweetness. . . This desire, which makes him maul, tear people from sleeping bags, so cross, so desperate. This is no children's story. This is a nightmare. The next day, my son steps on horse manure my Sicilian mother says is good luck, because she wants to see a bear. I am compromised. Want not to see a bear yet want my son to have his wish, to have what he desires, I believe in desire. Is that why I believe in this bear?

This morning my father spots a rush of brown outside the trailer. My mother is ecstatic. She wants to see a bear, too. She and my little boy rush outside together to see this bear, knocking into each other, they run through the pine needles.

It is a raccoon. A big raccoon. But they are disappointed.

I try to understand this. Clearly the bear they want to see is just something wonderful, like a firefly, some furry emblem of wilderness, a presence that will make the trees and stars authentic.

The bear I don't want to see, the bear who searches for me even now as I lie here in darkness clutching my pan listening for shuffling and grunts is hunger, is desire, is terrible. It wants to tear people from sleeping bags, it wants to know, what does it mean to sleep, what are we, what does it all mean, as if ripping zippers, crashing windows, crumpling metal doors, overturning ice chests, marauding, would uncover secrets like worms beneath the stones, knowledge it needs now, now. . . It wants to know. It wants to know everything. I lie awake, waiting. It knows just where to find me. It's not just that you have the marshmallows and Oreos it craves, perhaps you do and have locked them in an aluminum chest. It's your dreams. It can tell. It can smell the sweetness of your memory, yes, images as crusty and short as croissants, warm with orange marmalade, and slippery with butter and raspberry jam, but more, your desire, it is drawn by the speckly Merced in you, glacially alive with trout swerving, its browns and golds and greens shimmering like ripples over pebbles in your mind. Your desires glitter, catch the bear's quick eye, and the bear cuffs through to memory trout holding their own, ripples in your heart.

And the bear's violent nuisance as we sleep, its vandalizing as it roams, wanting, wanting what is inside— locks, doors, zippers, snaps, these things we think keep things out, keep things closed: bears don't know the difference between side and top, locked door and walls, skin, and clothes, it's all the package meant to be unwrapped.

How foolish to think, as I have thought these past nights, of the bear, pausing at the tent flap, imagining the bear unzipping with padded fingers, long claws, delicately grasping the zipper prong, only enough to swivel its monstrous head with its red eyes, to peer into the tent to see what's tasty tonight, to find me, huddled in the corner, waiting with my pot, ready to clang, to shout, to rush out when this bear, this bear, could open the tent without using the zipper, could walk in without any flap. Just a rip and suddenly brightness a set of brightness of stars and eyes and perhaps moon, a growl, and an immediate smell in my tent cave, fur against stars. To think of its surprise, its fear, as it leaves me, clutching my pan.

Yes—yes—I want to see it— stooped and fat and fast coming round to see me poking its head in, its huge head at the zipper, its hand pulling wide the tent flaps—I will clank the pans I clutch; I will drive it away in terror, in both of our terror—wondering—me—what I have, what is marshmallow in my blood, brain, desire, memory, all, all I see, all I feel, when this bear comes—it's out there now, it knows just where to find me. I believe in this bear. This bear might kill me if I don't have what it needs, but I know my mother was right, I would be lucky to see this bear. Ah, bear, I wait, ready to be quiet, if you come.

From my journal, November 5, Hilton Hotel, New York City, At the American Studies Conference, five oclock in the morning, On the red staircase in the lobby:

I, I am the bear. I don't know quite what this means, now, here. Months have passed.

It is night still and people are sleeping. I don't understand so many things, I cannot sleep— this night hunger, wild hunger, my room useless, intolerable, room service has nothing to bring me, nothing I need. Worries and darkness and pockets turned inside out—this ice chest shakes, tears open—is it hope? Think of such hope!

On the Park Trail

On the park trail, my arms swinging,
I came upon a man, hobbling along.
As I passed, he called out, are you walking or running?
Well, I'm passing you, I panted, so I must be *flying*.
You're good, he said. Proceed.

Klamath Falls Next Stop

Is it snow there on the peaks?
A ditch reveals clouds lit with sunrise,
Red, pink, gray, and grace notes
Of rain on the train window,
Telephone pole, trailer and cow,
Fence, and thoughts of you
In this March of time.

Snow, heron picking worm
In puddle just released from ice,
Your eyes with Spring, new
Shoots, what a time you came,
And all of Spring is before us,
Its winds, its birds, its
Snow, rain, and sun, its melting,
It's freezing: this is your time.
I've been on the train all night.
As I write this,
Sun sweeps snowy hills
So grounded by night fog. A heron
Perhaps too dazzled by the sun
On its puddle, startles and flies
Upward, like a word on a page.
The train makes a low
Long howl. The coyote, who
Saw me naked last night, too
Dazzled perhaps by my white flesh

It thought was moon, leaped up
Into night's purple mist. There
Were stars, and snow, and now
Ice—or white water--
Or reflection of sky—
A ditch, a lake, a river, your eye,

The lens of you, as we
Travel over this land, float or fly,
Soon I will see you, a mirror
Of this terrain, this time:

This is what the Universe meant,
When it made Spring, and you.
Am I ready for this new life?
Next stop, Klamath Falls,
And the stops never end: us, together, now, soon.
Winter snow, spring rain, this morning.

Arctic Lilly

Last night I woke to drums,
Or I thought I did: maybe it was my dreams,
Drums pounding; I felt my way to the door,
Guided by sound—and overheard the Northern Lights,
Arcing and making the sky look bigger than I ever knew it was—
Louder in silence for spectacle rhythmic life.
How enormous is this world?
And perhaps the drums calling to me
Were my heart, perhaps the drums of the day
Called my heart into sync with sky,
Perhaps my heart is also arcing
And these colors are pounding
In the white bear, and trillium beneath the ice,
Perhaps Spring is pounding and the drums
Announce that sky is alive, Universe is happening
And young and circus and shenanigans and glitz and amazing.
Perhaps the drums and lights are in me, sure,
Called by the elders who know how to call the Universe awake,
Its pounding heart, its way of love, helplessly beyond, beyond
What any of us can know, but only hear and see and dream.

This Thing We Call Friendship Is Bigger Than We Know

Luna the whale aka L98 or Tsuux'iit, wanted only to be our friend. Every day, the Canadian Department of Fisheries and Oceans said, she got into trouble: the more she tried to engage us, the more she was an outlaw. Humans—Mowachaht/Muchalaht First Nation, journalists, teachers, tourists—were written up. What was their crime—and they did get fined—it was looking the whale in the eye. This was proscribed. By law, no one could relate to the whale. Ignore it. And yet the whale did not understand. It swam up to the boats, grabbed a hose with its mouth, and sprayed the folks on deck. It made all its entreating sounds. Don't look at it, people were told. Look away. You are robbing it from its whale-ness. It never can become a real whale and go back to a pod life if you allow it to experience humans as its community. But some came to believe that ignoring the whale was cruel. One man finally decided—he was a writer—Luna (he was a he) wants friendship. It was like Huckleberry Finn: I'll go to hell! I will look him in the eye. Come what may. I'm not going to say here that the government backed off, and that it was a happy ending. Well, it was a happy ending, but it is not one that saved the whale's life. They wanted to imprison the whale, cage it as a danger. The First Nation, the elementary school, used song and dance to encourage the whale to resist capture. It was a tug of war, engines vs. boats paddled by singers, government vs. the people. It was not we the people. A whale who wanted to be a friend broke down the boundaries of who we are as people, extending enfranchisement to species with a heart. A journalist who came for three weeks to report on the goings on stayed three years, called to friendship. He said, "this thing we call friendship is bigger than we know." It turns out we learn about friendship from a slippery and leaping creature, and that the possibilities for friendship are infinite in this universe. Luna was killed by a tugboat's propeller—the fishermen hated the whale and wanted it dead—but here we see, none of us who watched the news reports wanted this whale dead. We all felt we were its friend. We all cried to lose him. Our lives were changed. He was the friendship teacher. Oh, yes, this is the happy ending. We learned about friendship. Maybe that will save our lives.

The Landscape of Love

How in a flat world you rise up in a grandness of dignity,
gathering yourself into folds of wings. Graceful drapes of earth
you shape by your own strength, and who knows what fires are
within you, from deep in the world's molten heart, its iron secrets.
Rising stance, to a point, jagged and crooked and sometimes sing
covered with snow, how you are a peak seen off in the distance,
far but dominating everything: the whole world sees the sun on
you in mornings, your crags lit gold and pink, the shadows, and
the clouds that surround you, only you, hover—how you make
these clouds, your own weather.

You stop the rain, the winds are stronger when one is with
you, the air is clearer and there's a cleanness, a smell of pine,
something exhilarating. And there are storms, alone with you,
thunder, lightning, hail, and you need a jacket in your nights,
even under starlight. The stars are more, more luminous, you
can see their colors, more, more clearly, with you. What is it
like to love this mountain, to be loved by this mountain? To be
with you, this mountain, is to be slightly breathless— walking is
harder, everything is harder, which means one's heart is working
harder, it's pumping, pounding, stronger. Your mountain is
resolute. It stands, in mystery, a force of landscape. Knowing
you is a way to know earth's passions, its volatile seethings,
its aliveness beneath its surface. Sure, as an eagle I would fly
to you, find a nest in what you nurture, your trees and lakes.
Sure, as a lion I would tread on you, safe and satisfied in your
being. As a cloud, I would be drawn to you, with my rain and all
the good things I have in me to make things grow—we do this
together, the team of us.

All of this is true, how you are mountain in my life.

But then I think you are the river really. Yes, the swish of you, the prance, the splash, the spray, the fancy way you have of moving, sometimes calm, reflecting blue sky, Green willow, the rainbow trout in you visible, the may fly luminous, and sometimes you are white water, a category 4 or 5, difficult and scary to navigate, requiring skill, courage—and is there greater excitement? The thrill of you, the energy, the way you capture and entwine the light, its gold, its shine. You move, quiet, slow, then fast, sometimes so fast you turn into a waterfall, and over I go with you, in the spray and roil. I sit on your banks and see the beauty of you. Sometimes you are so big I need a bridge over you, sometimes you are so narrow I leap over you, and the best part is your pebbly bottom, and the birch leaf that floats on you, like a log, and the heron that thinks it owns you, and does.

But really, you are Paris. Not even so much the city— well, yes. Of all the towns and cities in my world, you are the City of Light, best and most joyously seen at night, when you are lit up, and all the ways of you, are lighted, and you can see your infrastructure, the complexity of your buildings, the arcs and circles, gentler curves in stone, the striped awnings, plaid bright chairs, the sidewalk cafes, the clouds over the Seine and all the beauty inside the amazing beauty that holds them, of course this is you but more, you are the going to Paris.

In my life of making it all work wherever I am, blown to the places of my raw fate, I go through mundane and terrifying everydays. I drive or am driven to the airport. Lane changes, trucks, stress of packing and decisions. of what to wear and learning what still fits. Getting out of the car or bus, do you see what I mean? At the curb, lightheaded. Carrying and hoisting. Lines. Worry in the scramble where is my...Security. Walking and carrying. Lines. Waiting. Holding. Checking. Boarding. In the air—in the world's trembling hands. Bounced...squeezed. And then get off the plane and it's Paris. I have forgotten to look at the world in the process of living in it and making it work in all its improbabilities. Suddenly there is sky, and it is beautiful and blue. There are rooftops and I am looking and feeling I am here. This is what it is all about and for.

Well, do you see this is a metaphor? Of course you do. You are with me all the way. It's you who said to write you a poem. Well, you didn't say it. But when I think of what I have to bring you, of what I am doing in residence on this earth, with this body and heart this time, it's to live a vision of yours and of you, to be here in this way. You are my destiny, my destination person, the Paris of my world, and whatever it takes to get to you, whenever our lives make that possible, those moments of being together, it is worth it all. Being with you, its arrival, at a place of beauty the world is proud of and in which I am excited to be human.

Meditations

I

Hello river who is I
You are moving along
With joy and vigor
I sing along with you
My best self who knows all the notes,
The choir of good news from the trees,
The rocks who love your moving over them,
Your caress.

II

Dear God, what do you want me to do with this shining world
You have given me, this breeze?

How can I serve You?

What gifts you give me, for my eyes, my senses.
There is purpose in such joy! I know.
How can I do justice to this, rise to this occasion?
I will be glad in it. I will rejoice.
I will give thanks. I will figure something out.
What to do. What to bring.
How to show how I am changed by this beautiful mercy.
This merciful beauty.

III

Being alive
But not more than—
In fact, showed up by —
The birds first of all,
Whose exclamations and calls and important flutterings
fill me and still me to a stunned agape of being on a bench
absorbing magnitude far beyond consciousness.
Or compared to the squirrels who race and startle and
stumble and scamper in tumults of gold and scarlet and green
long grass in stalks staked by sun so loud and singing I unfurl.

Yes I am a poppy in such company,
And the bees believe in me, alight and weigh me down,
Until I spring back, open to whatever happens
Here in the wind.

Part Six
PRESENTS OF MIND

If Marvelosity Is *Not a Word*, Then How Do We Know What It Means?

For my purples at CSUMB and Armando Arias

On hearing that the Earth has five billion years left before being extinguished by its mother star our sun, our solar buddy, oh Earth!

This is different from what the astronomers predicted yesterday: that in twenty-nine years an asteroid a mile long will hit us surely and end most of life on earth. This is different from what James Havelock predicts of the billions of lives to be lost in the next fifty to one hundred years due to climate changes we have caused (when I hear this, I automatically am counting the years my children will still be alive, will they be there for this or that cataclysm?).

I get out of the car, holding my coffee cup, nursing my headache, it is still early morning, and I have driven my daughter to school. I look up at the pine tree next to the house, and a blue jay is on the branch. As my gaze travels up the trunk, up and up, like Jack's Bean Stalk, higher and higher, I see the blue sky framed by branches, and a little way off, an almost full white moon.

We, humans, may not be perfect. Certainly this morning I do not feel a good specimen of health or wisdom. The world around at war, and people treated savagely. I myself cannot even prevent unkindness nor sorrow common as rain. We as a species, this generation, ignore the science and we ignore history and we ignore the wisdom built up over time, against all the odds, all the odds that have ever existed against finding out, understanding the complex marvelosity of this happening world. It has never been easy to know. Was it not the Tree of Knowledge from which we were not to eat? That idea has been around a long time, and yet it took billions of years for us to develop to the point where we were shaping stories and inventing ways to count, to see, to express. Philosophy, science, it was all one. And it came from looking at the sky. It came from standing on the soil or rock and looking at a tree. It came from getting wet in the rain. It came from hunger, seeing plants grow and figuring out from the moon when they would grow again.

It is so simple, looking at a pine tree with a blue jay on a branch, seeing a white moon in the pale blue morning sky. Oh earth, we love you so. We do not want you to die. Us, yes, it is all right, I do not like it, and I am finding it hard to bear even one death. Even in the sunlight golden on the marsh with the blackbirds on the orange stalk their sudden startling red which you see when they take flight, stopping your heart even as your mouth opens in awe, opens in rapture, sorrow sits on my tongue, it eats at my ear, and I crumple like a bag, as if I have no bones.

We could imagine comfort in any of our deaths that we rejoin our earth, we become part again of soil and rock and sky, we become bark and reed and yes, even blackbird wing, we are the smoke arising from the campfire, we are the scales of the fish winding its silent way in the cold clear water that looks gold, and earth, earth lives, earth is eternal, not this tree always, perhaps, but trees like it, trees forever.

And so I look around this morning, too cranky with my headache even to talk, I look at the leaves, in a green shape moving as individual leaves, and as one whole, I look at the sunlight lighting up each leaf, I look at the trunks, each so complicated, and the way each limb goes its own way; I look at the amazingly different kinds of trees which grow on our planet, after a time of nothing but gas, then water, and then the miracle of soil, and seeds, I know nothing about this, I cannot comprehend how we got trees. How can it be that earth is fated to die, like a tree, like any of us? Like a star? For when our star takes out this earth, like a bee stinging, it goes out too, its explosion is what will eat us up. And this makes me realize that I am just as sorry for our sun, nothing is like earth, but the sunlight, it is our longest known happiness. And now I know, of course, that this light on green blue earth is indivisible from the sun, and when we lose the sun, we lose the earth, and it all is back to one starry, starry night, full of more suns and probably earths everywhere.

But I wonder, I can't help wonder, if the Universe has anything like regret, or wistfulness, in a Plan in which this earth was grown, this particular earth, this way of living beauty, and will disappear, or become like Mars, a rock with a memory of seas and who knows, fish and the dragonfly.

In that same time, more than 15,000 people were killed by lightning; 4,000 by bees; 10,000 by deer; 1,300 by rattlesnakes.

SOME FACTS ABOUT MOUNTAIN LIONS

Even though half of California is prime mountain lion country, these animals are rarely seen by humans. In general, mountain lions are calm, quiet, and elusive. They are most commonly found in areas with plentiful prey such as deer, bighorn sheep, raccoons, rodents, and other small animals. They usually hunt alone, at night. They typically cover the carcass with leaves or branches and may return to feed on it for several days. Though they are most active at dusk and dawn, they can be seen at any time of the day. Mountain lions are solitary except during mating.

It is due to their secretive and solitary nature that it is possible for humans to live in mountain lion country without ever seeing a mountain lion. The potential for a human to be killed or injured by a mountain lion is quite low compared to other natural hazards. It is more likely that a person will be struck by lightning, for example, than of being attacked by a mountain lion. Over the past 100 years, records show that only 13 fatal mountain lion attacks occurred on the entire North American continent. In that same time, more than 15,000 people were killed by lightning; 4,000 by bees; 10,000 by deer; 1,300 by rattlesnakes.—Brochure at Visitor's Center, Garland Regional Park, Carmel Valley, California

Wilderness n. savage, ferocious, frenzy, insane (Webster's Dictionary)

To know you is to know the range of danger of the heart. *Secretive, solitary, calm, elusive*: it is possible to live with someone without ever seeing them. We live with mountain lions, it is said, and it is safer than lightning (my terror at which you scoff), and you, you love lightning. You love storm, its shattering sounds of wind giving itself utterly to its impulse of velocity, of pent-up energies from its time as star, as light. (As I imagine the lion leaping, although I do not know yet from what source is its spring.) You love the bolt, the flash, the universe breaking apart, a crack into the light that is there behind and beyond any darkness in our sights.

It is said that living with lions is safer than life with bees. And you love the honey, the sweetness, you love the hum of bees, their presence meaning that something is near that you love, something growing, fragrant, and thinking of this you hum, too, and sometimes, if someone nears your wings, interrupts your dance, your secret way of knowing where the good things are you might sting—a way of lightning and leap, a way of wind. Rattlesnakes, of course: their sinewy paths, like the river you love to see meander through the marsh grass knowing a heron is nearby and bass below. And deer: you love the mystery of these creatures that stand so straight and so still, carefully stepping, eyeing everything, knowing without looking what is there. The deer don't care. Without seeming to look: their peripheral vision. The things you love that frighten and kill, the things you love, still. You behold the lightning, and you are thrilled to see the snake. The sound of bees, and the quiet of deer, is worship, and you say you want to see the lion, you go at dusk with your hope the lion will appear to you. All right then. I unhinge the prayer for safety, I lift off the leather tie on the corral gate of my fears, to let in the knowledge of a startling universe with energy to spare, or perhaps let out the knowledge—let it spring, let it kick, let it burn, let it sting. As dangerous as it seems, this world, loved by a man who loves living with lions, and me, too, me, loved by this man who loves danger, I let go the value of safety and I say roam and wander and love everything that is wild and free, the way I know that you love me. The way, mortal risk aside, I give my heart to you, of course, I would not live any other way, for the sighting of you! You, in my wildest dreams.

Another part of the heath. Storm still.
Enter KING LEAR and Fool

Be forgiving like the rain which never gives up on us.

Be still as you lie on the bench under the shaking leaves while a
lion watches you.

Let your eye mirror the sky and your brain be full of flight.

Keep in mind the words of birds who flock in waves of letters you
can read.

It is true the universe is barraging you with wisdom messages, as
it appears.

You know the eyes that watch you watch for you, for your love.

Like the bird who rides your belly swell, let your white wise head

    Be loved

        By me,

            Not a lion,

                But who loves you just as much.

What's Your Story, Morning Glory?

A 66-year-old woman on earth reads the news. There is news and there is news. One is the news perhaps of men dying miserably or living miserably—against what Dr. Williams says about poetry, "the news without which men die miserably every day." I have been reading the news of our planet earth from the newspaper. Potatoes have been taken off the do not eat list and approved as something you can eat once again if you are a pregnant or nursing woman on food stamps, as, although it is starchy, the potato has potassium and fiber. But not French fries, they make that distinction. Other news. Meningitis has been found in a student and all her fellow dorm-mates and classmates are being notified. A train coming out of Grand Central Station that goes along the Hudson, one of my favorite train rides, lyric scenery that makes you want to become a Hudson School painter yourself, or watery-eyed poet, crashed into a Jeep Cherokee and killed the Jeep's driver and six people on the train, which burst into flames. Harper Lee is publishing her first novel, after 50 years, amidst disputes that it will not be as good as *To Kill A Mockingbird*, since it will not have the same editing or any editing at all, and her sister who just died at 103 said Lee could not see or hear anymore after a stroke that made her move into assisted living, the words of which take me instantly in a neural dive into indignation and sorrow and remorse and fury and despair and guilt—adding insult to injury, the isolation and humiliation and loneliness of ending one's days with strangers in bleak and dispiriting rooms and cold hallways—yes, in which our mother lived (miserably). I would have done it so differently. I live this over and over, and how I would have rescued her. Then Chuck told us that he and Doris were going to move, to some kind of senior facility as they no longer can deal with their house, and this was a shock, and I tried to talk them out of it, we have been together in each other's lives and did Lamaze together and see each other's comings and goings twenty times a day, and bring each other soup in all occasions of falls, pneumonia, crises, and Doris said, "this is not a house for old people." "You are not old people," I said. "But we will be," she said. I do not get this. I probably refuse to get this. I am a refuse-nik person to this. Today I would go and drag mommy out of that assisted living to be with me, even though she is afraid of falling out of the window, taking her away from where she is safe and clean and cared for. And I will now know to say, all right, I can live with that. Because that is what she would have wanted, did want, and no matter how messy, I would have her with me. And I would have driven her to Yosemite, too, for her 90th birthday, even though I could not lift her and we both would pee in place. I would have some bravery and spine. Where was I, yes, so, Harper Lee. So I think I could teach a course on Literature That Changed Minds, and include her *To Kill A Mockingbird* and its sequel now, *Go Get A Watchman*, and *Uncle Tom's Cabin*, and *Civil Disobedience*, and John Muir, and *Invictus*, *The Fire Next Time*, and other mind-moving works. Perhaps Lee's book did not change minds, but immediately I began to think of ways to teach the two ... maybe a course on how literature responds to social issues, and include this and Stowe and Walter Miller, Jr., *Canticles*, etc. And so the news, yes, I'm turning the pages, and a Jordanian fighter pilot downed in Syria is burned alive in a cage. I was thinking of Joan of Arc, the young woman burned alive for insisting that God was with her, for having a more personal relationship and more encouraging relationship with God that informed her inspiring leadership, someone everyone was afraid of, even the French for whom she was fighting, terrified at the idea of the power someone had who can invoke encouragement.

Sometimes I am afraid of what our Creator thinks reading the newspaper. I want to spare this God, say, don't look, God, like Adam, I am ashamed, to think of God so sad to read of the cruelty to people, to animals, to earth itself. Because behold such a beautiful earth, such wonderful minds that I get to engage with every day, in this blessed work of being a poet in residence, teaching, such struggling striving minds that I get to know as a teacher, such enduring love and loyalty of mind that I get to know as a mom and wife, such sweet caring minds I get to know as a sister, as an aunt, such goodness of minds that I get to know as a friend, as a member of our community. And from here, this morning, as I write this, is the news without which men die miserably: I look up from this table, where I sit in the green leather chair from some estate sale Christer and I hiked to in the snow in my overalls in Indiana for White Cow Pasture so many years ago, and there, in the lightening gray that is morning, a squirrel swings from the birdfeeder, embracing seeds in rapture, and now right here, camellias blooming, three, and buds, in early February, the earth knows something, feels something, of growth, of resurrection, of renewal, of improbability, of resolute determination to carry on as beauty—this little sign, this little red camellia, its own news, this poem of God, written in fog, and which I read, drinking my pumpkin coffee, looking up from the morning stories.

A Poem for Christer in the Coming Spring

Write me a poem, you say, about this, as you lie on the picnic table to bathe in the sky, to watch the leaves sprout on the tree, green, blurry with life, yet not your favorite time, you say, when there are more leaves, and then they are touching each other, and that is what makes the sound in the wind, the leaves together.

So, I listen to you, and look at the tree.

We walk on an ancient path, by old, old trees, whose branches still attached fall to the ground, lie along the ground. Branches in wild grasses.

What you really want to see is a mountain lion.

You watch for it, you walk in the twilight when you may see it, and you know it is watching you, all this time, and first it saw you walking, and limping, and looking, then slowly jogging, and walking, and then finally running, but always looking, and then walking again, and lying under the tree, under the sky.

The lion likes the way you go to nature, what you want from it, why you are here. What you listen for. It keeps watch on you for me, looking for you to appear, like the tree, in stages, blurry with life. It listens to you, your silence. Yes, it's here, watching you, hearing you, in these lines, with its big feet, and its calm eyes, and it loves you, basking in the sky bath, it loves you in these lines.

Be Mine

Are you loved? If you're needed, that's a clue. Think of how you are needed. By earth, for example. Earth needs you. Earth goes all out for you. It dishes up sunrise, it plates sunset, for example, every day, chocolates and roses, the original delivery service, messages of be mine, I'm yours, outlandish and lavish displays for your notice, some peacock's tail spread—yes, yes, it wants to mate with you, that is for sure. Maybe not right now but some time, some celestial dazzling union. Or reunion. It needs you to be impressed, and amazed. It needs your poems of notice. It is your beholding eyes that spring the rivers, your dances to its strings and wind instruments that pulse the tides, your obsession with lemon pie that grows the grass, your love of light on seas that makes it tilt and spin and spin and spin and spin. That is how much your sweet heart, your wondering eyes, your grateful ears, are needed. And that's just earth. One example, how you're loved.

Bones and Flesh, cont.

For Glinda, Lightworker, on Lighthouse

I have no idea how to think about my body, some stricken landscape.

Your touch.

At first, I'm plains, buffalo, hump, hunched, then hands find tree roots in my shoulders, shake and free burls and stumps in my spine, gnarled, nests in my neck, boulders in my upper arms, and I find myself feeling grateful I have a back, that we are covered with flesh, even our skull, we are draped with flesh over rock, I breathe lavender and pine.

My flesh is river, a wild Merced, flowing over rocks, I am moving, a current—and then my bones begin to sing, my shoulder sags and droops (I am a ribbon, untied, a present to be opened.) My bones are music, and my feet are on the line; I pick up my cell phone, who is this? It's my toes, and my arches, who have grabbed the phone. Now everyone is talking, thighs, muscles, knees, ears, a waking up like sunrise and the birds.

Perhaps I am a field, and the wind moves through me, and then, suddenly, silent and it is just me, this slab of solace, and hands never stopping, instructing the pain, my flesh is listening to these firm hands. I keep my eyes closed, imagining myself whatever it is—not these bones and aches and flesh— just the warmth, that is all I am, just the warmth—in a sea floating like kelp, moving with the current, light. How ancient is this practice, laying hands on another? It is as old as wind in grass, and I am flowing. I keep my eyes shut, and feel light, light, I think, light is what a geranium knows, and light is being when you no longer are heavy as stone; and no longer own the pain and the stiff struggle against gravity; light is a dolphin carrying me, no longer flesh and bone, but buoyant spirit, warm, warm rising in the morning sun.

Q & A

Sitting on the balcony on Forrest the Bear overlooking Amtrak parking lot, a nice morning office, Austin skies for ceiling and walls, interior clanking, and wind.

Here are the questions. On being ill. On discovering that you can get better.

I am scared.
That seems not to be a question, but it is a question.

I am sad.
This is a question. Will I be sad? What if I am sad?

What if I become healthy and I still am sad?
That is a question.

There are answers. But they are to even better questions. There is asking.

When the trees wave their branches, the skies say, oh, they are asking for rain.

When squirrel scampers up the tree, it asks for seeds to carry home.

When the flower becomes purple and unfurls, it asks for your eyes to see it and say, how beautiful. It is demanding. It asks for your happiness.

When you worry, what will become of me, you ask for something the world has got in its pockets and is glad it carries it around for such occasion.

What is that, mommy? What does the world have for me in its pockets when I lie awake with worry?

The world says, ask me, ask me.

When the trees wave their branches, maybe they don't know they are asking for rain. Maybe they are nervous, maybe they ache. Maybe they hurt and lack water. All they know is, they find themselves in a flutter. We look and we see vibrancy, we smell the sweet greeny fragrance of their dancey aliveness. We don't know what they are asking or that they are asking, and they don't either. We say, how lovely they are, and they feel misunderstood. But the skies understand what is being asked here, and they send rain. And the tree feels answered for a question it didn't ask. Although, see, it did ask.

So, when you wonder, when you worry, when you lie awake, you are asking for something that the world will know how to answer.

The Case for Unreasonable Faith:
Peace Lanterns, at Lovers Point

Words for the Peace Lantern Ceremony Pacific Grove

When I think of what will redeem our earth, when all that we do, how we raze and slash—(not you, no, not you)—makes it seem like no worth, how we poison and deplete what grows and all the matter of earth's life, not only mountains who are scalped and bowels exploded, not only the lion and the fox stranded, the bird poisoned and what else flies, but people everywhere, in all our strife, how we're shot and maimed—when I think of the woes to earth and everyone, yes, I think of you. I think of what glows, I think of a peace lantern lighting up the dark and giving hope to a world that thinks somebody sees me, somebody knows. I think of the hope you represent to the spirit of the world; I think of what will redeem our earth, and all of us—a peace lantern sent forth to give us this message bright and clear: do not give up on us, O world.

This when the flying news comes in, the landing on Mars with cameras to tell us what we already knew, that water existed, surely that life was there, before they cut down the trees, before they stopped listening, because now there's you, Dr. Seuss, John Muir cheering at the news today that the Sierra Club executive director got himself arrested, chained to the White House iron fence, on behalf of a pipeline protest, good for you, good for me, peace lanterns hurtling on this planet of ours right now: there are souls, hear me now, earth, who hold you dear.

The Geology of Peace:
Otherwise, I Would Not Dare to Hope
For the Peace Lantern Ceremony Pacific Grove, 2014

The birds know exactly what you are doing, and why.

It's for them, they know. The earth knows better, but it's just as glad,

A bird, a species, a people, each precious and miraculous, spiky, and difficult,

Complicated, and so worth what it takes for peace:

To have any part of it safe, humane habitat—

Because peace on earth comes like this, one mind, one soul at a time,

Casting our lot with everything coming together, land, sea ....

One look on this cove, at each other, and you have all you need to know.

The sea can tell us all about why we are here,

Why we care about peace, I and you.

When things are so difficult up at the store,

So boring and heartbreaking and so much to fear,

Joints are so stiff, when it's worse to read the headlines than have the flu,

What's at sake in this turbulent world at its core,

Where things are hard, a build up of what has been broken,

Breaks, over and over again, hard things, erosions of what seemed

Relentless and forever, where immovable mountains are hurled,

Collapse, yield into stones and then sand, and pieces of forests,

And creatures with and without eyes,

Strewn and littering, smashed and smooth, from crashing,

Crashing, and yet, see one crab on the rocks, the white crane,
    riding the kelp,

The gull, striding the air—we're floating on a memory of
    catastrophe,

And earth counts on us, you and I,

Because we're the ones who see this as beauty,

Who look on this with love.

If we are quiet, shh,

We hear the flow of life.

The barking of our hearts,

The pulse of brainwaves telling us all, all we know.

Surge, in this briny send-off of hope,

We stand where people have always stood,

Where life itself began, in this intersection

Of moon power on earth, earth's surrender

To forces of ebb and flow. We gave up our tails,

Our claws, our beaks: is peace possible, friends?

It always has been possible.

It always has been the case that people gather as now,

To send off our best hopes, our knowledge shining,

As clear as silver light on water, as golden light, on sand,

As clear as the sight of you, standing here, caring.

Resurrection Shenanigans

On the sighting by scientists of fox thought extinct,
Caught by remote cameras leaping orangely
In the manner of e.e. cummings' leaping greenly trees

> *i who have died am alive again today*—e.e. cummings
> *Be like the fox: Practice resurrection*—Wendell Berry
> *Shaking it over here, boss!*—"Cool Hand Luke"

I praise gods fox can read because what the poets say may
help. Fox and us, if there's a difference, our redemption and
their resurrection.

Trees are poems the earth writes. Of course, says His Insouciance,
who is the first Forest Professor, holding the Alpine Chair. He
loves Kahlil Gibran.

Why, asks the fox, using the Socratic Method, the one he
taught Socrates in the Grove, do you think there is such
excitement in the sight of me, leaping once again on the high
slopes? It was blurred, but I heard a scientist wept at the
photograph.

Yes, squirrel? (I'll have you for breakfast later.)

The squirrel rises to the occasion, cannot help being a good
student, even though it costs him his life.

Well, from the Buddhist perspective, adds the fox, life here,
life there, it's all flow. You'll be grass, or me, tomorrow.

You'll live again, just as I have, despite (you endure this too) human hunters and hungers, the quest of skins and tails and stew, charging forests with knives and nets and guns, as if our forests were an enemy camp.

And the trees, abiding wild life, aided and abetted: guilty as charged, and we saw them hung.

People danced on their stumps, left them to rot, like carcasses of buffalos slashed for their humps. We hid, like outlaws, those who lived, in what forests were left.

Yes, squirrel, you have an answer for this morning's news, the sight of us? That one, perhaps two, might have survived, if eyes do not deceive, might love indeed, someday as common as grass?

Question from squirrel: did you say *love?*

No, I said, *live.*

All due respect, you said, *love,* anyone reading this poem can see that plain.

That isn't even grammatical, your mind is squirreling. And I wouldn't say love is common, even if you *could* say "love common as grass." It is as rare as a rare red fox, sighted in alpine heights. (Ah, indeed, live, love: loved fox one day be *common as grass?*)

I wonder, says squirrel, Professor Fox, no, this is me asking,

squirrel could not conceive such question, to what you
attribute this joy in your leaping presence once again in our
world? Our hearts leaping Wordsworths to behold a rainbow
in the sky?

Says fox, not that I think it is deserved good news, totally, that
we may yet live; not that you deserve the glory of the sight
of our fur, a red cloud, orange current rushing in the grass,
always a blur, but the trees can say. The trees stand for us,
rooted and flying, *live, love,* trees think it's simple, the same
thing, what can't be without the other, says Professor Fox. If
you need me, if you grieve me, listen to earth, singing about
me in trees.

I've always lived in poetry, adds the fox, I'm Hughes thought-
fox, I'm Rich's dream, Clifton's "dear," tutor of The Little
Prince, sleep of Merwin, I'm in Khartoum in 2006 with Al-
Saddig Al-Raddi, even the moralists, Aesopian, citing my love
of grapes, like you, Poet, by love of chickens, like you my wise
guy ways (hey hedgehog)—

Wait, you said, says squirrel now, *by love of chickens,* did you
mean, *my* love of chickens?

I said, *my love of ....*

No, you said, *by love of ....* It's here for all to see.

So I step in, the writer of this poem, on the news I read of
scientists sighing, I mean sighting, I do mean sighing, too:
Sierra rare red fox spied, who have died, alive again today, not

all dead, giving us now another chance to let them live, in their
crafty ways: what am I saying, another chance for us, to *love*,
I mean *live*, I mean *love*, I do mean love, well, live perhaps by
love of, our crafty leaping love of, this world's fox-loved nests,
whir and wings: love, learning earth's wild voice that speaks in
trees, and fox in us, we who live poetry.

Called Upon for a Poem for the
Day of the Dead Ceremony in Pacific Grove
Artisana's on Forest, November 2, 2012

You have to. You're the city poet.
It's a ceremony to honor one's ancestors.

Ancestors? I don't know any ancestors.
I am so out of water here.

I don't even want to think about it.
I am too squeamish.

> On remembering my ancestors,
> Through the lens of my grief, my missing them—
> The mornings I still want to call.
> The anguish of seeing them frail, diminished in body—
> I could not hear them, they could not hear me,
> My missing them in my every day, so much.
> How did I let them go?

I am tearing up.

Oh please!

They don't like this.

How dare I even try? But—what, darling, don't you like, my remembering you?

I don't want you to think of me as DEAD.

This is my mother.

How can you say I am frail? Who was chopping wood the day he died?

My father is not happy either.

Ah—okay—how would YOU wish to be remembered?

Not like that—

Together—the one thing they agree on: *You and your poetry! Come on, now!*

And since when are we ancestors? Is that a way to speak of us?

I change course.

> And images parade in a circus of proud elephant
> moments,
> life's sequined ladies and lions,
> a red and white striped tent of memory, with peanuts
> on the ground—

What are you saying here? What peanuts? What is an elephant moment? Can you try to see us? How we were?

I squint at our life.

We had good moments! Or what was it all for if you don't remember?

I remember.

> This jolly crew in the morning, at our campsite, my father
> in his cowboy hat making trail cakes, he called them, on
> our Coleman stove, with pears and onions and bananas
> and bacon, ooohh we say, but he's so pleased with
> himself, how resourceful, using our supplies, he doesn't
> get mad when we shudder with disgust, so ungrateful,
> he's SO pleased, his eyes are happy, green gold as the
> shining Merced full of trout, and he shaves in water
> where ice formed overnight, showing off his brio, and gets
> pneumonia, but he doesn't regret it

I didn't regret it! And I didn't die!

> He's full of vigor, and exuberant, bringing my mother,
> shivering in the morning cold, hot coffee. Coffee, Jerry,
> she moans, wearing his down jacket in the one camp
> chair he brings for HER (we sit on logs or the bench at
> the table), and he's so glad to be of service, his breath
> visible in the air, in the light now streaming through
> the trees

*You did bring me coffee, although what were you thinking, we don't
need five dozen eggs!*

And I'm laughing at their antics in the middle of their lives, an
everyday moment, nothing for poetry, nothing for the picture
books, just a moment when we weren't even thinking we would

all live forever, but just ... living, in red shirts, flannel, and warm voices! A life of morning gifts!

Oh! I am so happy.

> One morning, I am in bed, the door opens, and it's my Mom in her bathrobe, Barbara, she says, breathless, awed, her voice alive with day, feel in my pocket. I am groggy, what? Usually, she is a little cranky in the mornings, but her voice is full of wonder. Feel in my pocket! I get up, put my hand into her pocket. And I feel a warm chicken egg.

This is from Old Red! Her first!

> This must be from Red, our beloved chicken she has raised, since I brought a duck home from school, imprinting it for my psychology class; it thought I was its mother, and followed me, going, beep beep! I brought it home and Daddy made a roof and water system, and we got a chicken. And my father got a frog, Vita, he held up in his biology class, illustrating his opening lecture, What Is Life, and my mother, in her first garage sale, is asked if it's for sale, and he says at the end of the sale, where's Vita, he's not in the pond, five dollars, Jerry, she says! I can't believe they gave five dollars! And it was he who said, when she wanted to have a garage sale, but we need the garage!

When you stop the wah wah— yeah, how it was. Yeah.

I have to think of my ancestors, not in the ways of sorrow, but as they lived, funny, and difficult, and charming, and generous, living as naturally as if life belonged to them, loving the stars and the campfire and the songs and us, hopeful every day for things to get better, for things to stay the same, for us all to be safe.

> Yes, I can see you—vibrant, wearing red, sitting around the table; yes, the things you sewed and painted, the pictures you took, the furniture you mended, the sculpture and paintings you did with oil, you two, in midlife, alive.

Oh, you guys!

I get it.

How would I like to be remembered, O my children, as your Ancestor.

Mommy, I can't really think of you as an ancestor.

Yes; think of me right here, tonight, feeling so lucky to be with this poetry community, so moved by each person's story, having such a good time, plump and limping home perhaps, as happens these days when I'm on my feet, bouncing and bounding around, I was so happy being with you I forgot; think of me here, this night, alive again today, this Day of the Dead, with my Pacific Grove neighbors, and forbearing beautiful Zeusy husband who wants this joy for me, think of us tonight, when we get home, having a bourbon over ice, and watching

Doc Martin, and eating leftover Halloween Candy saying we
shouldn't, and worrying about YOU, O our children, remember
us alive ... remember everyone alive, not in sorrow, like John
Muir, dying of a broken heart over Hetch Hetchy Valley being
drowned for a water tank for San Francisco, how, John? He said,
when I was sixty, I had been sick, and there was a mountain, I
promised Louie Wanda I would be careful, just take it easy, but
before I knew it, I was on top, shouting, The Glory! The Glory!

That's how I would like you to remember me, as I lived.
And so, as your future ancestor, O children, remember me, in
these lines, remember our times as clowns and angels and fools
and earnest, worried, prayerful, and hopeful and so happy when
you call; think of me, having such a good time.

O ancestors

She means us, Jerry—

whom I love and honor, in these lines, you live, you love,
you cook, you sew a button, you come through, you are jaunty,
you make coffee and drink it leaning on one foot, you sigh and
say, how can you die. You read the poem of your poet daughter
and sigh, and you will always live here, you will always be alive
here, and so loved.

Who knows if this is a poem—but I think we helped her out here.

I Write This Anyway, Despite, Despite, for People Unafraid to Wave

For Patricia

events must be sung and sing themselves—R.W. Emerson
I celebrate myself, and sing myself—Walt Whitman
i who have died am alive again today—e.e. cummings

I

In the middle of our life, a dark woods where so much that once we had is lost—what fills me with grateful awe that I'm here—as much as the forgiving sound of rain on the roof, a crow's laugh in the morning—is a train horn, a sweet whoooo, that transforms the moment, makes of my life right now a concert, and my desk the front row for the orchestra of earth, the song of something going somewhere, on its own journey of purpose, and I'm feeling part of that mystery that is the unseen train, its way of moving on earth, clanking humbly through backyards of tire swings, of leaning not-yet-collapsed shacks weathered colorless (more beautiful than a company headquarters), of people unafraid to wave, our true selves, our best selves, a song knowing us, our backsides, our wrinkles, as alongside leaping trout approve a fellow journeyer making its way and heron stand one-legged in ditches, puddles reflect an incomprehensibly whole sky of clouds and geese in formation: notes someone can sing, and the toot, the hoot, the way of hello—how lucky am I, how wealthy we are, we who live in the flight path of rain, of heron, of train, of crow. In its own way, a train horn, a daily newsfeed of what the human mind can do that turns out to be ... beautiful— in the way of someone with whom you have lived a long time—a joyous message of what we have here still and is not lost. Some things are still here. And so we find ourselves in the sound, together: we are not lost; we are here to hear it—we are here for each other, in the darkness, called, here, and now, in the perfect present.

II

I sit, reading my phone. The noisy sea below catches my attention. Don't look at your phone! Look at me! The sky says here is top of the hour news; the rocks shining with water in the afternoon light so bright it is black and white say this is what's trending. I have forgotten what I have to worry about or dread—all the dismaying news feed. Earth says read me, look up, oh, look around! And I realize I am wondrous—there is happiness yet in me; I am still green inside this moment.

III

I am sitting here aging my skin by the pond after all the winter. The sun lures dragonfly and me, fellow fliers drinking in the light. The water too—its shine says it all. We cannot tell each other enough, what it is, to live in this luminous world.

IV

No moment is without the world, even here. What is being asked of me, as I sit on this bench by the pond in the afternoon breeze? No one is here, in the silence, except the world, a busy bustling calliope of minds and hearts, yet no voices, except the world's voices in my head, and those heard right now of every tree, its own voice, grass stalk its own story, bird its own tune. Surely, they are asking very much of me, if but I knew. Only the train knows—it sings its song. Only the waves, coming and going. I sit here in what feels somehow like quiet to me. The wind in the trees sounds like a river. A bird sits on a twig very still, and I believe it knows me, it knows my dead son who is alive in this bird's world and it has come to tell me this, to sit with me, in silence that is not silence, in a place where I am doing nothing, except noticing, all the ways I am called on as I sit on this bench, if only I knew.

V

What a little miracle is a pond or for that matter a ditch, a drop of water that contains sun whole and five hundred thousand stars, that draws a bird, a winged insect, that contains a shining fish and undulating worm and clouds and rain, weather, whole weather systems, rocks, sounds, a frog, and most of all a heron who stands as if he owns it. Which he does. The marsh grass that curls at the top. The willow. The swoop of the hawk. The glide of the soaring gull. The universe's magic mirror. It peers and holds up this image of itself preening, wondering if it has wrinkles, if the gray shows, how it's aging, but all we can see is beauty, thrill, and miracle, so maybe this is where universe needs to look, maybe this is the true role of poems—our awe and wonder, our sense of amazement and happiness in a little wind wrinkling the face of water and sun wrinkling my face which the world sees as its own face, and thinks is beautiful.

VI

And we who feel broken, we who feel lost—who have lost, like our earth, ninety-five percent of original groves—a time when we and our world inside and out once were bouncy and green and emergent—now diminished and frayed—or gone; so much has happened to our hearts, torn and weary, to each other and our earth—and yet, here we are. We look at what we are part of, what is still here. We are the leaping dolphin, the standing heron on the kelp, the backyards no one sees, monkey flower and grevillea messy growing out of the discarded washing machine, the people unafraid to wave (who cares what anyone thinks, who cares if we are judged, uncritically waving on whom and what we do not know, just waving at what comes and goes, like the train, like the waves, like our fate. We squint in the light; we peer into all nature as a pond, a sea, that sees us, the wilderness in us yet).

This Poem Is Written Commando

I'm Nobody Emily Dickinson said, and it was more than
what the sly Odysseus meant to escape the Cyclops. I know
what she meant, now, because I cannot find my underwear
… any underwear, I cannot find any of my underwear, I am
writing this commando. I don't know why I am telling you this.
I don't know if you have ever read a poem whose lines were
authored commando. (Are you saying, ahhhh, can you tell?)

One day this part week, in fact, graduation day, this is what I
could not find. My graduation robe. My Ph.D. hood that goes
with it. My underwear. My earrings.

Today, visiting my mother in hospice, I have lost my journal. I
don't know where I left it. I drove 45 miles back across town,
and it took two hours, this is Los Angeles, west side to east
side, and over the mountains in the middle, to go back to the
store where I thought I left it.

This is the most naked feeling of all—a journal does not wear
underwear. I think it has to do with the magnetic belts, and
these are things that are re-absorbed by the energy fields.
But I wonder if it is seemly for a sixty-four-year-old woman
to be losing all her underpants and going around without
any and telling you this. How not lost but hopeful it is when
everything is leaving you like Mars' seas, how you become
Nobody and now and marvelous and everything is possible,
and no one knows.

Scurrilous driving home on the streets lined with jacaranda
in full purple bloom, astonishing against the blue sky, trees
purpling the grey pavement, filling gutters as if the Caesar will
ride by, and I think of Alice Walker, what she said about the
color purple, and I think of God, and how on the TED talk
of genius as the muse from without, from the gods, asking
you to write a poem, believe in the world asking this of you,
and is this something in the realm of the sacred that I should
write. Certainly, it is what I am thinking about, driving home,
in my parents' Impala (its own sad story), the two guys next
to me not knowing that I am commando, and this is what I'm
thinking about, how is it that this same mind whoofed by
sacred call of muse is commando and no one knows, how we
are called or in what state, no one ever knows when you are
commando. But it changes everything.

Why I am telling you this. Elmore Leonard: delete the parts
your readers skip. Everyone will skip this part. Except you.
My editor warned me, my mother begged me. But here you are,
with me, after all. Present, perfect.

Addresses to the City on the Poet's Address

April 23, 2010
Statement to the City of Pacific Grove of Dr. Barbara Mossberg, Pacific Grove Poet in Residence

I'll tell you something very funny and wonderful about Pacific Grove and this appointment. Is poetry practical in these days of civic crises? Is it an extravagance, optional, a luxury we cannot afford, a time-waster in these demanding and hurried times? But a doctor—an obstetrician—who had daily responsibility for life and death, thought otherwise. William Carlos Williams wrote, "my heart rouses to bring you news that concerns you and concerns many men. It is difficult to get the news from despised poems, yet men die miserably every day for lack of what is found there." He would know. He saved lives by day, bringing new life into the world, and at night, he saved lives in a different way, writing poetry—and in the process, saved his own life, his own spirit of resilience.

He was not alone. Pacific Grove knows! Like eating, like walking, poetry is something people do for quality of life, for life itself. It is essential to nurture and exercise the soul and heart. But most people think that this activity is something quirky (charming but impractical) about themselves or people they love. No one owns to writing poetry. But if we x-ray a flourishing community, we find bankers, insurers, teachers, presidents, chefs, business owners, massage therapists, moms, mayors, airline pilots, artists, city council members, florists, electricians, for whom poetry is part of their lives. People write for joy or solace, to organize their thoughts, calm their seething spirits, focus attention on the divine, find beauty and truth and meaning in their lives, and send messages of hope and comfort.

But can you imagine a whole town making poetry its business? Pacific Grove has identified poetry officially as a civic function, a city service, part of its governance. Writers have been integral to its history and ethos. Its famous architectural preservation, its vibrant "Main Street" way of life, go hand in hand with its respect for the role of arts in community living.

Of course, poetry has supported and stirred civic spirit from the beginning of civilization, a way people originally came together. The root of civic culture, law, philosophy, business, ethics, religion, poetry has been at the heart of movements for democracy (including the founding of the U.S.), peace, war, civil rights, and activism on the part of the earth. It has played an indispensable role in civic life from our most ancient times. Poetry is the voice of the community as people gather around a campfire to share what we know, to listen to each other's stories and discover we are not alone. Poetry packages our knowledge and values, and in its lines is resilience for our human condition—there is grace, in forgiveness of ourselves, and there is insight, as we find new hope.

Pacific Grove is famous for more than its value of poetry; it is home to the Monarch Butterflies. I reflect that it makes sense the Monarchs should make their way here on their journey to a place on earth that values enduring beauty. No wonder this is the place where Poets are invited "to perch" in a house formally identified as "the Poet's Perch."

So, it is a special honor and excitement for me to have the chance to engage with this historic and iconic city to contribute to your vision of a poet in residence. I join in work promoting the practical necessity of poetry in a community committed to its continued vibrancy and resilience and respect for what a community can be in these hectic and confused days. Pinch me!

April 23, 2010
To Cedar Street Times

I've always been a poet and humored by various generous-spirited communities to organize poetic events. My job titles have been wonderful—President, Dean, Professor (the best of all), Scholar in Residence, Senior Fellow, Fulbright Lecturer, each an incredible opportunity to serve. But to have the title of Poet in Residence! This makes whole my various selves: thank you, Pacific Grove! In honoring me with this title and position, you honor each of your poets, the ethos of your community. You have many "poets in residence," and I will do my best to represent this amazing community of poetry-minded citizens celebrating the spirit and letter of poetry in our daily life. "Ink is dripping from the corners of my lips, there is no happiness like mine, I have been eating poetry"—Mark Strand. It is my hope to convey such happiness poetry brings to our city's life.

I saw PG as a civic model of creativity long before I came to live on the Peninsula. For example, in my federal appointment as Scholar in Residence at USIA and as ACE Senior Fellow, based in Washington, D.C., I designed and led a program to bring leaders to PG's Aquarium to see the role of language in promoting a civic culture of respect for earth—how the intersection of language arts and environmental and entrepreneurial interests worked, as a national and global model. And PG called to me like Bali Hai: I came here with the Society of Women Geographers, and stayed at Asilomar, and was so taken with PG's beauty that I put a continuous stream of photos of that experience on my desk as president of a Vermont college, a promise to myself that someday I would come to live. I was brought again to PG to speak to the high school, and to speak to the Annual Meeting of the Northern California chapter of Phi Beta Kappa, and to the business and arts communities of PG for various projects, my go-to place for walking, restaurants for birthdays, cafes for recession cappuccino, massage, nails and hair, hardware, paper, lumber. . . when I have manuscripts to send out I drive to the PG post office for luck ... .PG has already invoked several poems as odes to PG enterprises. So I look forward to learning from the poet's lens PG through and through, hearing its voices, and giving back in return new words and life out of myself that PG draws forth.

To the People of Pacific Grove
on the Occasion of YES on Q

Thinking with a Community on the Necessity of Libraries and
Books and Civic Spaces for Words
Through the Lens of Chaos Theory

What a privilege to explore with this evolved community
the topic of books' roles, how writers play leadership roles in
our society, roles that cause change in seemingly immovable
overwhelming systems. With enough time we could discuss my
other heroes who illuminate the power of a book to change the
world, Mark Twain and Frederick Douglas, and someday, our
poet president Barack Obama whose life was changed by his
exposure to poetry and his not only reading it but writing it—
who can say what other books he will write, and perhaps inspire
other presidents to write; who can say how daily reflection
impacts leadership thinking, conscience, resilience, legislation,
moral decisions. The fact that we are here in Pacific Grove,
founded with the Chautauqua spirit, Butterfly Town, USA, is
symbolic, it seems to me. Yes, poets always find symbols, but
consider this Event, a city devoted to our society's temples of
literature, science, and culture, the most fitting constituency
with which to draw an analogy from emergent physics, chaos
theory, whose emblem is the butterfly.

The Butterfly Effect is the name given for the theory that
even the smallest energy event is a disturbance, a perturbation,
that over time and space causes massive change in complex,
nonlinear dynamic systems. "A butterfly flapping its wings in
Brazil causes a cataclysmic storm system in Texas," as one of the
founding scientists put it.

As a cultural historian, I love this image, because it
expresses the reality of what I see in the case of writers to

change our world. If we think of Thoreau, for example, who died poor, sick, and unheralded, his "Civil Disobedience" essay ended up, over time and space, in the hands of Gandhi, who was inspired to apply it to the situation of his fellow Indians in South Africa. As an approach to changing society, it was so effective that he carried it to India, with famous results in the transfer of power from British colonial rule to independence; world politics changed. Gandhi visited America and our leaders. And as Gandhi became a beacon for peace and non-violence, Thoreau's message over time and space and filtered through Gandhi, circled back to America, to Martin Luther King, who felt that it could be applied to his people: so elegant in the symmetry, since Thoreau's activism was originally on behalf of slaves and the need for national reform of laws of human and civil rights. Thoreau's writing was a 'butterfly," migrating thousands of miles, causing enormous changes in our system of laws and in our culture that continue today. Dickinson, aka "I'm Nobody," is a butterfly inspiring strength and resolve and courage to endure and face life's greatest challenges, of immense solace and comfort and power to people around the world; John Muir's flapping wings of writings urging wilderness protection brought president after president to consider his message and create environmental legislation.

It is words, and their sharing, which led to the leadership skills and knowledge we have seen in these "nobodies" (and called worse) in their own society who today rock our world. Muir's writings led to Julia Hill taking up the name "butterfly" and staking her own life to save a tree, giving the tree a name, Luna—from the luna moth butterfly, to enable us to connect our own humanity with the earth's plants, and writing a book about her struggle that in turn led to an educational foundation, Circle of Life. Saving lives: life and death. Words? Listen:

"Of asphodel, that greeny flower,
I come, my sweet,
to sing to you!
My heart rouses
thinking to bring you news
of something
that concerns you
and concerns many men. Look at
what passes for the new.
You will not find it there but in
despised poems.
It is difficult
to get the news from poems
yet men die miserably every day
for lack
of what is found there.
Hear me out
for I too am concerned."

This poetry is by William Carlos Williams, part of "To Asphodel, That Greeny Flower." Life and death stakes in poems? He can't be serious—a poet's dramatic carrying on. Yet he should know—his day job was an OB-GYN, he was in the life and death business daily, and was a Pacific Grove type person, he would have loved knowing he is being quoted here tonight with you Grovians in a library: his poem credits his insight into the news we need, the news that could save our lives and change the world, with books—

We danced,
in our minds,
and read a book together.
You remember?
It was a serious book.
And so books
entered our lives. . .
Of asphodel, that greeny flower,
I come, my sweet,
to sing to you!
My heart rouses
thinking to bring you news
of something
that concerns you
and concerns many men. Look at
what passes for the new.
You will not find it there but in
despised poems.
It is difficult
to get the news from poems
yet men die miserably every day
for lack
of what is found there.
Hear me out

Ok Dr. Williams, we hear you, in our mortal garden, revealed as a butterfly. And does it not make sense, the physicists' way of describing unlikely power in the universe, as the flap of a butterfly's wings? For the physicist it is the wind those fragile, yet might wings generate force. Yet here in Pacific Grove, we have another way of understanding the poet physician of the cycle of life as a butterfly in his poem. Grooving pac-grovy gardeners know that it is the butterfly, who is not only an emblem but a true lover, whose sexy visits to a flower is the catalyst that lets that flower be a force of co-creation in the universe (E.O. Wilson said that without them humanity could not exist more than a few months), and the butterflies—who are smart and outlived the dinosaurs—know a good thing when they see it—they obviously know that civic-ally and culturally speaking, you are the cat's meow, the butterfly's object of desire, this community, adopted by the winged symbols of growth, this community who loves books, and libraries which are book preserves, to which we come in the role of butterflies in our community garden, transforming us, catalyzing the power within us to grow, change, soar ... so that nobodies with book's power can change the world. This is the home ethos you create in your support of libraries and books and the life and death news that is within them, that nurtures us, with godly nectar, and so it makes sense to me that Thomas Jefferson, who never wanted to go without a book around—he was so anxious about being without a book, heaven forbid, that he placed them strategically around the house, so, waiting in the parlor to welcome a guest, if there is a minute interlude, he's got a book on the mantel where he's standing—he said he had a "canine appetite" for books, and it was his library that was the foundation for the Library of Congress, for he could not imagine the nation he conceived in liberty, with the conviction that all men are created equal ... and endowed by their creator with inalienable rights among which are life, liberty, and the pursuit of happiness, without access to books: the library was the quintessential cornerstone of the democratic society; and that when Mark Strand, a poet laureate of the United States, for the Library of Congress, in our own time, is in the library, he finds himself panting like a dog with Jefferson's canine appetite, saying, "ink is dripping from the corners of my lips/ there is no happiness like mine/I have been eating poetry." And thus, books nurture the butterflies in all of us, and this is the rousing news we need, long live our libraries, the preserve of butterfly hearts and minds to change our world, and keep it alive and well. Emily Dickinson, our favorite "Nobody"—who wrote about butterflies, conceived us as butterflies dining on tasty authors and soaring to Somebody-hood: books saved her life, and made her life, her immortality, so that she lives with us today: Let's give her the last word:

> He ate and drank the precious Words—
> His Spirit grew Robust—
> He knew no more that he was poor,
> Nor that his frame was Dust—
> He danced along the dingy Days
> And this Bequest of Wings
> Was but a Book—what Liberty
> A loosened spirit brings—

It was poetry that liberated Dickinson so that she was free in this world, so that it was a residence, a placed she lived fully.

> There is no Frigate like a Book
> To take us Lands away
> Nor any Coursers like a Page
> Of prancing Poetry—
> This Traverse may the poorest take

Without oppress of Toll—
How frugal is the Chariot
That bears the Human soul.

Each time someone takes up a pen, picks up a book, walks into a library, he or she may be launching the powerful butterfly effect, no matter how poor—how marginal and outside the Beltway and politically fluttery one may feel. Each time one takes up residence. Each time we engage a book we are butterflies stirring the air, the ethos. Reading and Writing are ways to engage powerfully, to take on, and up for, the world, in conscience and courage and hope. For the friends of the library, the home of the Poet in Residence, community activists on behalf of literacy in our lives, it is especially fitting for those of who live here in a pacific place and on the path of the butterfly migrations. As you are nourished here in each other's company and then go forth from here in Pacific Grove, you express the power of the butterfly, in each of your ways, the questions you ask, the thoughts you generate, the actions you take, to help us live up to the legacy of the greatest minds, who, as long as we have had language, are on record urging us to peace, to do good on behalf of groves, of each other and our earth. In joining you these past years, I salute you and clap for the flap that I see going on here in your support for a library and schools and poets. You are the butterflies, and God bless you. So thank you, Friends of the Library of Pacific Grove, for this honor to be your Poet in Residence, with you, in this hallowed library, surrounded by books that are civilization's butterflies, and we don't know where it can lead, when one picks up a volume, but we do know it can make us feel at home for the present. Go well, butterflies. You're flapping and I'm clapping for you.

Speaking of Poet's Address: A Word at the End
Majesty of Grace on 18th Street

From my journal of Life in the Poet's Perch:

> *Continued from my brown paper journal, wet at the bottom from my shorts when I went into the pool, writing on a chaise lounge. Not my M.O. but a way to see the sky—and realize how to see the sky is perhaps what we are supposed to do, how we always have read the Universe. Now it is afternoon, I have driven home, walked up to Grove Market for a tomato, split pea soup, two cans of tuna, and to the bakery for sesame bread and a macaroon for Christer, and made tuna salad and walked three minutes each way to the bench by the Swan Boat, and thought more about what I was writing this morning and my community of leaders writing in journals and making To Do lists from New Year's Resolutions and I resumed my journal on this computer, not yet getting back to Work, thinking of walking down 18thth Street:*

I may not know your name, you who sweep your porch, and you, who paint your fence that bright white,

and you who carry the pitcher of water to your rose bush, so that it blooms by the sidewalk, and provides a whiff of sweetness as one walks by. . .

acts that give our civic space a style and us a grateful sense of presence in our world. Was it your resolution to do good? Who knows where our habits, our sense of obligations, our resolutions lead?

You, of these gestures, do you know how someone is thinking of you, when all is said and done, in the consciousness of sorrow, and loss, of bad manners and bad luck, of what is frightful and tedious and fraught and disturbing (we see the faces of drivers, we see the faces when no one's looking, how it is, and we can understand).

I am thinking of the word *whiff*, and *scent*, and *sniff*, and how to capture what it is one feels walking, with unexpected news of something clean and cared for and beautiful in this world . . .

Okay, I am not saying there's a certain heaven, but you can see in the scheme of things what you did, it's the little thing *you* did, you gave what you had, when it mattered a lot, and it was majesty you made, something important in the mind of someone looking back and realizing that all is not lost with the world, and you never know, do you, just when the Universe will reveal itself to you as something generous and good, some whiff of passing grace.

The gestures not on anyone's To Do list for New Year Resolutions that no one taught you to do—the wealth that you have that no one knows and is not on your bank statement, and will not help you get a loan, the uncounted, uncountable sweetness of you.

You are the source of a blessed life, you are the agent of the Universe, you are a vision of angel, a way people forgive and know from this glimpse into the divine, this whiff of—I'm not saying there's heaven. This is in you to do, and you, at the end of the day, are a new beginning, in what is remembered.

I'm not saying you will be glad if you do these things, watering your rose bush, painting your fence, you may not be or you may not think twice, and go about your day, but someday someone will think of you as evidence of an infinite world

The resolutions alive in you who sweep your porch, and you, who paint your fence bright white, and you who carry the pitcher of water to your bush, by the sidewalk, and provide a whiff of sweetness as one passes by, and slows, stressed thoughts startled by interrupting rose.

Who knows where your resolution ends and someone's hope begins, a new day, a new way? What we can learn from being with one another, a kind of news of kindness aloft and core to this world.

On this beginning of a New Year, mounting the threshold of going forward, I am reminded of how we create structures in our lives like in a poem, with beginnings and ends.

We make ends to make amends, we make ends because we want to make new beginnings, and structure our time and lives like stanzas, always a chance for a new fresh start, like our sun each day. I suppose this is why our earth turns. How ingenious of the Universe, a whole system designed for new days and starts ....

As I look forward to this new year, I think of the lessons that carry me forward, and the first one is the understanding of how it is *our* earth, our community, our time here, that being in each other's presence on this journey has taught me. A community alive with poetry is a way of civic grace, of kindness, listening to poets' spiritual devotion and practice. And so, I resolve in this new year to read and honor what's here, what's made anew, trees, and poetry, and music and dance, and mountains, and love, as never ending, and always beginning ... our community of such life, in the perfect present imperfect, the view from the poet's perch.

Acknowledgments

It takes a village. I am grateful to the Mayor and City Council of the City of Pacific Grove, and the City Staff, and Board, Staff, and Friends of the Pacific Grove Public Library, who make possible the logistics of the position of Poet in Residence in the midst of all the gritty and complicated business of managing a city in the limelight and all its institutions. I am indebted beyond measure for citizens who have taken up the cause of poetry in the civic space, grounded in the Pacific Grove Poetry Collective—Marge Jameson and the *Cedar Street Times*, Cathy Gable, Susie Joyce, Karin Locke— gifts, genius loci, treasures to community. Their visions of what a poet in residence is and can mean have generated and sustained poetry as a living presence, and are responsible for this book landing in the hands of Patricia Hamilton and Pacific Grove Books. Lisa Maddalena, Diana Godwin, and Laurel O'Halloran, encouraging city voices cheering us on: each in specific ways and together have been generous with time and resources to build a program around poetry that serves the community. The Poetry Collective's shenanigans on behalf of poetry include but are not limited to designing and carrying off events at the Little House at Jewell Park, the Gazebo at Jewell Park, City Chambers, *Cedar Street Times*, Motorcycle Museum, Pacific Grove High School, First Fridays, art galleries (including Flash Mobs at Artisana and Pacific Grove Art Center), Pacific Grove Public Library, forming a chapter of the Emily Dickinson International Society and related events involving artists, musicians, visiting and local poets, generating a Rumi Society, Burns' dinners....

Many people and institutions have supported this five-year experiment in civic life, including Walter Gropius and the folks at Canterbury Woods, Steven Silveira, Mary Turk, and the Pacific Grove Public Library, Teresa Basham, Karen Sharp, and the Carmel Women's Club, Robert Reese and the Cherry Center for the Arts, directorial dynamos Rosemary Lukes and Walt de Faria and civic gold, Michelle Crompton and the Osher Institute for Lifelong Learning—all the OLLIEs, Jeanne Adams, Patrice Vecchione, Patrick Flanagan, sustaining civic arts, Dr. Bonnie Gisel, Curator, Yosemite Conservation Heritage Center (former LeConte Memorial Lodge), Yosemite National Park, Larry Roberts at the Lilly Arctic, Milt Cox and Gregg Wentzell at the Lilly Conference on College and University Teaching, Professors Pam Baker and Dr. Dorothy Lloyd, California State University Monterey Bay, Charles Goodrich, Springcreek Project, Oregon State University, Markku Henriksson and Mikko Saikku, University of Helsinki, William Copeland and Terhi Molsa, Fulbright Commission, Finland, Dr. Yolanda Robinson, U.S. Foreign Service, Hal Ginsberg and Sara Hughes, KRXA 540AM/Radio Monterey, Zappa Johns, podcast Barbaramossberg.com, the *Monterey Herald*, the *Monterey Weekly*, *Carmel Pine Cone*, California Central Writers, Larry Haagqvist and Poetry Out Loud, Robert Marcum of The Bookworks, Pilgrim's Way, the Original Bookies (Barbara and David Ehrenpreis, Janet Meier, Bonnie Clark), UCLA Department of Biochemistry and poetry supporter Dr. Cathy Clarke, the Emily Dickinson International Society, the International Leadership Association (and Fetzer Institute), the Fulbright Alumni Association, John Muir High School Alumni Association, Goddard College, University of

Oregon: vibrant ethos forpoems in residence. In the putting together of this book, the Colrain Conference with Joan Houlihan and Tupelo Manuscript Conferences with Jeffrey Levine and Kristina Marie Darling, were transformative. Ah, my family whose being makes me present, and whose presence—on earth and heaven—informs these poems—Christer, Nicolino, Sophia, with our crew for these carryings on, their poetry and sense of what is at stake in its being written, Steven and Cathy Clarke, Will Clashe and Connie Ann Clarke, Lorraine and Steve Young, Stephanie Rose Young and Neil Bailpayee, Brian Young, and Madeleine Faith Young. Glinda Anderson, a good witch, on Lighthouse Avenue lit my way, setting me on this path of residency here for the present, Christine Crozier, and the immortal Fruitcakes. And in the midst of fires, pandemic, civic turmoil and Sargasso Seas, the Patricia Hamilton, genius loci Guardian of civic spirit for whom poetry is an essential worker, and Pacific Grove Books, deus ex machina. Hoisted!

Citations

Foreword
Beverly Cleary, *Ramona the Pest*
Thornton Wilder, *Our Town*
William Carlos Williams, "To Asphodel, That Greeny Flower"

Part One
Emily Dickinson, "I'll tell you how the sun rose"

Part Two
William Stafford, "The Well Rising," "The Way It Is"
Raymond Carver, "Late Fragment"
Psalms

Part Four
"Alive Again Today"—from e.e. cummings
"i thank You god for most this amazing," in "Loafing and Inviting
My Ease" from Walt Whitman, ""Song of Myself," ("I loaf
and invite my ease"), *Leaves of Grass*, 1855

Conclusion
William Carlos Williams, "To Asphodel, That Greeny Flower"

Emily Dickinson, *The Poems of Emily Dickinson: Reading Edition*,
ed. R.W. Franklin (Harvard, 1998)

Some poems have developed in the Tupelo Press 30-30 Project
(a digital media format for a poem a day for thirty days); versions
also appeared in the following:

"Loomings," *Tupelo Quarterly* Launch Issue, October 2013,
*Sometimes the Woman in the Mirror Is Not You and other news
postings*, Finishing Line Press, 2015

"Ode to My BCBG Holy Inappropriate Dress," first published
as "After Pindar, Bon Chic Bon Genre: Ode to My BCBG
Holy Inappropriate Dress," *New Millennium Writings*, 2014
(Award, Honorable Mention)

"I'm Shaking It I'm Making It but the Woman in the Mirror
Doesn't Move at All," *Tupelo Quarterly* Launch Issue,
October 2013, *Sometimes the Woman in the Mirror Is Not You*,
Finishing Line Press, 2015

"Q and A," *Sometimes the Woman in the Mirror Is Not You, and
other hopeful news postings*, Finishing Line Press, 2015

"Day Break: Take This," *Sometimes the Woman in the Mirror Is Not
You, and other hopeful news postings*, Finishing Line Press, 2015

"I'll Tell You How the Sun Set," *Sometimes the Woman in the Mirror Is Not You, and other hopeful news postings,* Finishing Line Press, 2015

"This Thing Called Friendship Is Bigger Than We Know," *New Millennium Writings,* 39 Anthology, 2015 (Honorable Mention Award)

"The Grove Market, My Neighbor," *Cedar Street Times*

"Poet in Residence," *Cedar Street Times*

"After A Meeting of the Pacific Grove City Poetry Committee," *Cedar Street Times*

"Washing the Lake," *Ammulehti,* June 21, 1989

"Book Me, Sir: John Muir Takes a Sauna with the Naked Ladies of Kuopio," published as "John Muir Takes a Sauna with the Finnish Ladies of Kuopio," Abbie . Capps Grandprize Winner, Olivet College, 1992

"What We Bring Home," *Ten Years of American Studies: The American Experience,* Renvall Institute, University of Helsinki, ed. Markku Henricksson, 1987

"Loafing and Inviting My Ease," [as "How I Am Taught Green], *Passion for Place*: Community Reflections on the Carmel River Watershed, ed. Paola Fiorelle Berthoin, RisingLeaf Impressions, 2013

"Willow," partially in *John Muir: Family, Friends, and Adventures,* ed. Sally M. Miller and Daryl Morrison, University of New Mexico Press, 2005

"The Case for Unreasonable Faith: Peace Lantern," *Cedar Street Times*, 2013

"Again: The Geology of Peace: Otherwise, I Would Not Dare to Hope," *Cedar Street Times*, 2014

"Resurrection Shenanigans," Exhibit: International Competition, "I READ THE NEWS TODAY OH BOY," Poet Laureate Program, Benicia Public Library and Pacific Grove Public Library (traveling exhibition of California Poet Laureate Program), "Resurrection: on the sighting by scientists of fox thought extinct, caught by remote cameras leaping orangely," 2011, 30-30 Project Tupelo Press, *Sometimes the Woman in the Mirror Is Not You, and other hopeful news postings*, Finishing Line Press, 2015

"I Write This Anyway, Despite, Despite, for People Unafraid to Wave," portion published as "We Who Have Lived in the Flight Path," *Eugene-Register Guard*, December 22, 2017

About the Author

Actor, playwright, dramaturg, cultural diplomat and entrepreneur, Dr. Barbara Mossberg walked into Pacific Grove's City Hall to be interviewed for the Poet in Residence position, reciting, "Ink is dripping from the corners of my lips/there is no happiness like mine/I have been eating poetry," words from U.S. Poetry Laureate Mark Strand. Sharing poetry about exalted experience in downtown Pacific Grove, she stated her goals of a "no place safe from poetry" civic culture: "Everyone becomes a "poet in residence," to know and express everyday momentous moments. She wants people to say about their lives, "Pinch me."

This interview summarizes Professor Mossberg's distinguished career of four decades as a prizewinning poet, author, and teacher, and honored educational leader, to promote the transformational role of poetry in people's lives. President Emerita Goddard College, founding Dean California State University Monterey Bay, Professor of Practice at Clark Honors College, University of Oregon, and American Council on Education Senior Fellow, she has been recognized by National Endowment for the Humanities, American Council of Learned Societies, Mellon Foundation (Aspen Institute) and others, twice awarded the Senior Fulbright Distinguished Lecturer. Committed to arts activism in the public sphere, she created and hosts the weekly hour Poetry Slow Down (podcast Barbaramossberg.com), and publishes in journals, newspapers, Huffington Post columns, restaurant reviewer, books (Emily Dickinson: *When a Writer Is a Daughter* was named Choice Outstanding Academic Book of the Year; Sometimes the *Woman in the Mirror Is Not You* and other hopeful news postings was chosen for Dublin Writers Abroad), keynotes, organizes lit crawls, poetry slams, civic celebrations, and arts fundraisers, and serves boards for the environment, education, drama, and the arts. Her roles as scholar, writer, and poet "in residence," include her federal appointment as U.S. Scholar in Residence for U.S.I.A., representing American letters in over twenty countries, Writer in Residence at Thoreau's Birthplace in Concord, MA., and Pacific Grove's California laureate Poet in Residence at the Poet's Perch, for which she says, "Pinch me."

A Word on the Illustrator

Sophia Mossberg has been a present in my world for more than thirty years. It is clear that she has been present in our world. Sophia has been an actor and singer since age 3, a writer and poet since age 4. She studied at the Stevenson School and Barnard College, Columbia University, and William and Mary Law School. Former prosecutor for Douglas County, Roseburg, Oregon, she is Assistant Attorney General for the State of Oregon. Her day and night job as an artist has brightened our lives since she first broke up a crayon to find its color.

— *Barbara Mossberg*

Printed in the USA
CPSIA information can be obtained
at www.ICGtesting.com
LVHW020733141223
766374LV00004B/216